DOLLY DISHES IT OUT

SHE'S SIXTY, SASSY, SINGLE & WAITING TO BE FOUND

Dolores (Dolly) Winston

Dolly Dishes It Out,
She's Sixty, Sassy, Single & Waiting to Found
By Dolores Winston
Printed in the United States
ISBN-13: 978-1719441940
ISBN-10: 1719441944

Editor: Karen Bearden
Cover picture taken by, Jean Szegedy & Dave
Pflieger, Bad Chicken Photography
Location of picture: Colonial Theater in
Phoenixville, PA

Dedication

To my wonderful family, mentors, faithful friends and my community, I want to thank you from the bottom of my heart for always being there for me as I created lots of "relationships" along my life's journey. You were always there to jump on board my ship. You all played an important part of the eight chapters of my life.

First, I give honor to GOD who is the CAPTAIN of my ship and at the head of my life. HE has blessed and given me favor in so many ways. I am humble and grateful for the opportunities HE has afforded me. I am a vessel to be used by GOD to serve His people. With faith, I am ready and willing, and I understand my true purpose is...
"HERE TO SREVE".

I am blessed to be the woman I am to today because of ALL of YOU. I am sharing my formula of how relationships in your life can be the key of how to grow and be successful. "When we bond with others is when we improve the quality of life".

Now I am ready to bless and serve others in a way that will catapult me to my next journey.

Acknowledgments:

Special Thanks to My Beautiful Mother, Yvonne Winston, and my sister, June Boswell. I could not have done it without their support. They were there for me when I had my daughter at 15 and had to finish high school. To my other siblings, Patricia Winston-Bellinger, Victoria Haynes, and Jay, Ken and George Winston, who were also there with me through every new venture and project I hosted or created. Thank you to my faithful daughter, Yvonne Winston, and my grandson, Carlas Rich, who have been the joy of my life and the reason I want to build a legacy to leave behind. I love my family dearly, and they have been my rock that has helped keep my life on track. I also have a special cousin, Neal Saunders, who has always been there for me in every way. I do not ever remember him saying no to me for anything I ever needed him for. To Donald Coppedge, an awesome life coach, mentor and father that I never had. This girl, now woman, could not have been more blessed than to have someone like him be part of my life. To the late Rev. Thelma Smith who became my Spiritual Mother/Mentor that taught me by example what is was to be a truly humble Woman of GOD. I truly love and miss her, but I believe she is smiling down from heaven with pride seeing the way I turned out. She helped me speak with faith, and that was her true gift to me. She said, "What comes out our mouth has the power to bless or hurt, depending on the kind of faith or lack thereof, showing belief in our purpose in life." To Karen Bearden, my classmate and friend I grew up with. She shared that she wrote Love Letters to Jesus and blessed me with a poem entitled, "Be Satisfied With Me". This poem inspired me to start writing my Love Letter to JESUS every morning. To the amazing women of Bethel Baptist Church who were my childhood role models and mentors who have gone home to be with GOD: Mrs. Debbie P. Mitchell, Sunday school teacher & Choir Director; Mrs. Arcola (Kitty)Thornton, Mother of the church; and Mrs. Ruby Armor, Deaconess and Spiritual Leader. To five powerful women in the community: Lois Gould, Karen Coldwell, Anna Mae Gailbraith, Doreen Passoff and Regina Lewis. These amazing women helped build my self-confidence in what GOD blessed me to do in my community. You never know what impact you can have on someone's life. I am here to share my journey with you. I am writing this book to tell my story, to inspire and encourage, and I pray that it will touch your heart to want to help someone and bless them the way I was blessed in life. We are "Here To Connect".

TABLE OF CONTENTS

Dedication...............................3

Acknowledgements....................4

Chapter 1   Lil' Miss Dolly...........................7
             "My Childhood Journey"
Chapter 2   But I'm Not A Bad Girl...........18
             "My Life As A Teen Mom"
Chapter 3   Still A Mom...............................34
             "A Single Mom – My Twenties"
Chapter 4   Mom-Preneur...........................65
             *"A Struggle But Living My Dream –
             My Thirties"*
Chapter 5   Health And Wellness.............171
             *"Developing Wisdom – My
             Forties"*
Chapter 6   Celebration Of Life.................212
             "Here To Win – I'm Fifty!"
Chapter 7   I'm Sixty, Sassy, Single and......254

Chapter 8   Here To Connect....................258
             Reference Books.....................275
             Contact Information................277
             Testimonies............................279

Chapter 1

Lil' Miss Dolly....My Childhood Journey

We all know that this wonderful thing called life is a journey and, oh, what a ride it has been for me. "Dolly Dishes It Out" is for you to feel and read along as we connect the pieces of my life. I love to cook and bake pies, and I'm hoping that as you take? pieces of me, you are intrigued by every bite. My prayer is that the sharing of my life might be a sense of hope for you and will help you understand the necessary parts of the ship you will need to build your life. Parts like mentorships, friendships and relationships, because we need each other to survive. My life outlines just that, a life with lots of twists and turns. But, at every turn, someone was there to be a compass leading me to the next piece. So take a bite and enjoy the pie as I begin to share the connecting pieces of my life. There are eight slices of my life I will share with you. Let's start from the very beginning......

The first slice is my childhood. My life begins as a young black girl who was born in the late 50's and grew up in the small town of Phoenixville, Pennsylvania. In those days, Phoenixville had a small minority population and not many that looked like me. We had a few minority business owners, and this little girl dreamed of owning her own business. Yes, I did. I dreamed of being an entrepreneur at a very early age. I can remember back when I was around seven or eight and dreaming of owning my own ice cream parlor. Everyone knows I love ice cream. I thought of all the flavors I would serve but mostly loved the idea of being the owner and serving ice cream to all my customers, especially the neighborhood friends. I was going to name it Dolly's Ice

Cream Parlor because I loved my nickname, "Dolly". My cousin gave me my nickname because she thought I looked like a little doll baby. The name stuck with me all my life. You really don't know how important it is to have your name be something you can be proud of. It is your identity that molds and shapes who you are. To this very day, I am known as "Ms. Dolly".

Now let me tell you a little about my upbringing. I was raised by a hard-working single mother. I am the middle child with three sisters and three brothers. We had a good life. We ate well and were warm, and we had new clothes on the holidays. My Mom would go to the local clothing store in town and lay away things so that we could look special on the holidays. We attended Bethel Baptist Church in Phoenixville, where most of my family are still members. Next year, our church is celebrating its 100 Year Celebration. My mother was one of the first members of the Sunday School at Bethel. This is where she developed her Christian foundation, and this was the foundation she brought us up on. We did not have a lot of material things, like a car or fancy furniture, but we had a great foundation with a loving, hard-working mother who was our role model that always wanted the best for her children. One of my fondest memories is going to Sunday School. Of course, my mom made it mandatory, but it was ok because not only did we get foundational experience through our Christian faith, but we got fun rewards too. Our favorite reward was getting to go to the yearly Sunday School picnic. Oh boy, what a great time that was! We couldn't wait for that Saturday in August when the picnic was scheduled. The church would rent a bus, and my mom would be up all night frying chicken and making potato salad for our lunch. It was a free trip to an amusement park like, Willow Grove Park, Dorney Park, Hershey Park, etc. It was an awesome trip for the family, and the only one we could afford to take each year. The whole time on the bus going up and coming back was a lot of laughter and singing. We really enjoyed it. These were great memories, times together with my family and friends.

My mother worked most of her life at Pennhurst State Hospital. She loved her patients, and she would allow us to visit her job so we could experience of what life was like for her at work. She would share many stories about "her kids", that's what she would call the patients. They called her mom and she responded like a mother. That was evident in how she interacted with her natural children.

My mother shared that we were blessed just to be normal children, with no defects like the children she spent her life caring for. One of the things that she taught us was to accept differences in other people who were unlike us and who had disabilities. I have always admired my mother for her work and passion and for the loving care she gave to other people. I know that's where I developed my true passion in life for loving and accepting others who are different. I carry those traits within me today as my mother still has that same loving and caring spirit. In 2016, she received the Miss Kitty Care Award for her years of dedication to serving and caring for others. My mother's heart is big, and she raised us well. However, some things happened in the raising process.

My mother worked overtime when she could, and those extra hours helped to get us those new outfits for the holidays. When she worked extra hours or days, she got a married couple to watch us. My mom knew the couple and trusted them, but what she didn't know was that the husband had a thing for little girls. I remember the day that would change my entire childhood and especially my view of men. I was eleven years old, and I remember being molested by the husband. One day as he was having his way with me, his wife caught him. She was very upset and yelled at him. I was in shock and very scared. She made me promise that I would not tell my mother or anyone. She said if I did, she would kill my mother and me. I never did tell my mother or anyone else, I was too afraid. This woman was mean and not very good looking. That made it even scarier. So, I kept it to myself and tried to be normal. Needless to say, they weren't our babysitters for long. I was happy and felt I could try to live without fear again. Then about a year later, when I was about 12-years-old, I was raped. Yet again by an older man who lived in my community. He came by my house drunk when no one was home and he raped me. And, again, I did not share what had happened with anyone. I was scared and living in fear all over again, and I kept it to myself. By this time, I'm not only extremely afraid, I'm also ashamed. How could this happen again? Why me? Is it my fault? Who do I tell? Will he hurt my mom? All these thoughts and questions were racing through my mind. The best thing, at that time, was to say nothing. And that's where it stayed, with me, saying nothing, until now.

In looking back at my life as a young child that endured so much negativity and pain, I realize I was a very strong child. I learned to keep things inside while continuing to push forward. Although at times I felt disconnected by fear, it was during childhood that I developed my sense of connection. I do believe in my heart that other women had these same experiences in life, but they did not and would not share them. My reason for sharing this is that I am free from the pain that I have suffered. My testimony to share is that I do understand the choices I made and the reason why I felt like I did. It has helped me become the person that I am today. Because of my experiences, I understand why I don't like being around negativity and things like drinking and smoking. Not only do they bring back bad memories, but the smells of alcohol and cigarettes actually sicken me. I understand where I get my strength from. The strength that was instilled in me early on came by watching my mom, my Aunt Esther, my grandmothers and women in my church work hard as they sometimes struggled taking care of the children and home while they helped each other get through.

I saw an episode of the Oprah show one day where they were discussing that I how it's possible to have a traumatic event happen in your life where you suppress it inside so long that it stays with you throughout your whole life. I never knew it was possible until I saw that show. We now know it to be called ACE's (Adverse Childhood Experiences). These experiences are potentially traumatic events that can have negative, lasting effects on your health and well-being. These experiences range from physical, emotional and/or sexual abuse to parental divorce or the incarceration of a parent or guardian. The effects are life altering that can cause our adult behaviors to be very negative. Very often kids who have

ACE's suffer from mental disorder, depression, anxiety, etc. Trying to deal with these adverse effects lead to substance abuse, alcoholism, physical abuse and many forms of negative behavior as an adult. The effects are much like the person who suffers with PTSD (Post Traumatic Stress Disorder). Learning this really explained why some of my behaviors are what they are today. Oh, but I have the grace of God that got me out of that experience and on to my next journey in life.

Chapter 2

But I'm Not A Bad Girl......

My Life as a Teen Mom

Then I became a teenager. How exciting was that! Well we got to move off High Street and away from the bad environment where we lived. The first project housing in Phoenixville was built on Fairview Street. Our family was blessed to be chosen for one of the 25 units that were built. Fairview Project was an opportunity where you did not have to pay electric or heat, and rent was based on income. The program was designed to help people save money so they would become first-time homeowners. My mother was finally at a level and in a position to do just that. We were so excited about the move. We had a playground, new furniture, and my mom finally got a car. Life was good! We were so

18

happy, and we ate like rich people! I can remember my sister, June, learning to cook on High Street because my mother got home late, and we did not eat dinner until 7 or 7:30 pm each night. My sister did a lot of cooking at our new home. I even got interested and learned from her. We would have full course meals and eat family style with everyone at the table. Sadly, that is lost in the life of families today. That was how families spent time together, at the dinner table. We had so many places delivering to us: Charlie's Chips, the Milk Man, A Treat Soda, and fresh meats from the local meat house. We were living well, and mom was saving money for our new home. Fairview Project's is where I got my first job. There were many families that needed babysitters with younger kids. I was blessed to be the babysitter that families counted on. I had six families that relied on me for babysitting. I was very excited and happy to be making money. I started my own bank account at the Industrial Valley Bank in Phoenixville. I was following in my mother's footsteps as she was saving for our new home. Fairview Project's was a beautiful place and a wonderful place for families to raise their children. I really enjoyed my time there with my family. Our next-door neighbor was Mrs. Ruby Amour. She became a role model and mentor to me at a later time in my life.

From age thirteen to fifteen, life was looking good for this young working teenager. I was babysitting and saving money for my big dreams. The dream of owning my own Ice Cream Parlor. One night while I was babysitting, an older guy who was nineteen years old and had a crush on me found out I was babysitting for his brother and decided to stop by. The kids were in bed and it was late. He was drunk and really pushy with me about wanting sex. I did not want it, but he thought I liked him and wanted it. Well it happened, and I became pregnant. He said it was not his baby. That was the beginning of rough seas for me. I had already blocked out what had happened to me when I was 11 and 12. Now, I had something that could not be blocked out. I had a child that I would bring into this world, and that changed the whole course of my life. I didn't want to make it bad for my mother since she was doing so well with saving money for her new house. Then everything hit her at once. One of my younger brothers was giving her lots of heartache, and she was at the end of her ropes with him. She put him out the house because he refused to listen, and he was only thirteen-years-old. Boy, did things ever make a turn for the worst. My mother was really going through when she started watching me and my sister who had just graduated from high school. She called my

21

older sister upstairs in the bedroom to talk to her about what was going on with us. At the dinner table, my mother noticed certain things that alarmed her that something wasn't right between me and my sister. So, my mother asked my sister what was wrong, and my sister starting crying. My sister revealed that she was pregnant and said, "so is Dolly". My mother was done after hearing that. She had just put her teenage son out, and then her two girls were pregnant at the same time. It broke my mother's heart. She was trying so hard to build a better life for her children and to have these things happening was not good. My oldest sister had graduated from high school, got married, and move out. She already had a child. So, this was going to be my mother's second and third grandchild. To make things more interesting, my sister was due in April 1974 and I was due in May 1974. I was working afterschool at the time I got pregnant.

It was at the Phoenixville Area Children's Learning Center on Main Street, and it's still there today. My hours were 3:30pm to 5:30pm. I would go to school, then to work at the Day Care Center, then I'd walk home to Fairview Street, about 2 miles each day. I persevered, and I was very determined to work up until I had my child. I remember it was Friday, May 3, 1974 when I went to school, then to work, and then I tried to walk home but couldn't because I had gone into labor. I had to get a ride home that day. My mother took me to the hospital twice, and they sent me home each time. After the third time, they let me stay until I gave birth to my daughter. It was not an easy birth. I was in labor all night. My daughter was born on May 5, 1974. Her father came to see her, but I was so angry with him, I refused to have anything to do with him. I was so hurt over what he had done to me and had nothing but hate for him, and I did not want him to be involved with my daughter. My Mother came to see her in the maternity ward. She asked the nurse to let her see the Winston baby, and the nurse pointed my baby out to her. My mother thought it was the wrong baby because she looked white. The nurse then turned the crib around so that my mother could see that it was the Winston baby, and she just could not believe what she saw. My mother questioned me again about who the father was. My daughter's father was already doubting her as his child, and now my mother doubted me too. I was so hurt knowing it only took one time for me to get pregnant. I was also so heartbroken that my mother did not believe me. My daughter was very fair skinned, and she looked white to me too. I didn't understand how she could come out so fair skinned when both her father and I were brown skinned. The nurse brought my baby in for feeding when I realized it was not my baby, she had brought me the wrong baby. I said, "Excuse me, this is not my baby." She then realized she had taken my baby to a white woman who didn't even realize she had the wrong baby. It was truly a mystery how that happened. I researched what Albino children looked like to see if my daughter was an Albino child. She did have the sandy brown hair like they have, and that almost convinced me. I have to say it was a shock because I believed that the way I felt about white people at the time was not good, and this was my punishment for feeling that way. That was a lesson I will never forget. People were always making comments about her looks, and it did not make me happy. I was just a teenager and a sensitive one too, and that was very hard to handle. I was in the tenth grade the year my daughter was born. I remember her crying all night and having to get up to go to school in the morning. It was not easy finishing tenth grade that year, but I did it with the help of my sister and my mother. My mother was very supportive and provided all I needed. We never received food stamps or government help because they said my mother's income was too high, but I was able to get free lunch in school. I always worked and saved my money, and that also helped in providing for my daughter. However, my mother was the major supporter of both me and my daughter. I can look back at these things now and see how far GOD has brought me. When my daughter was about six-months-old, I found out that my mother worked out a deal with her father, so he could visit her regularly. She didn't want me to know because she knew I hated him and didn't want him to have anything to do with me or his daughter. I am still paying a hefty price for that today. This is a lesson learned that I want to share with mothers who do not have good feelings about their children's father, and my advice is NEVER let your emotions get the best of you. No matter how bad he hurts you, children need their father and they grow up loving them and wanting to be with them even more. What my mother was doing made me realize that he had accepted and loved his daughter and wanted to be a part of her life, so I started to forgive him a little and allowed their relationship to grow. He would come and get her on weekends and spend lots of time with her. This has paid off for him, and he has been a wonderful father to her and she loves him dearly. I must admit, she has a better relationship with him than she does with me. I do understand that a father's love for his daughter is very different then a mother's love, and it happens like that sometimes. I struggled with that while raising my daughter in my younger years. It wasn't easy being a single parent. I still had to finish 11th and 12th grade while raising my daughter. I was not able to participate in school activities because I had to work. Although my mother was very supportive, she always reminded me that I was a parent with responsibilities and no longer had the privileges of being a teenager. Reflecting on those years helps me to see why I am so passionate about wanting to help young girls who experience becoming mothers at a young age. During my 11th and 12th grade years, I was in a co-op program where I was only in school half the day and worked the other half, but I was not preparing myself for college. I was just taking care of my daughter and did not see the opportunity for college in my future. Back when I was growing up, we were not exposed to many people who had gone to college, so looking for a factory, state or government job was the only way to go without a college degree. I graduated in 1976 and my daughter was 2-years-old. The only thing I had on my mind was getting a good job so I could take care of her. I was so thankful to my sister and my mother who were there for me so I could finish school and graduate on time. It was a true blessing in my life. I was always a go-getter, and three months after graduating I landed a job in a factory— Containers Corporation in Oaks, PA—only two miles from my home. It was a great paying job and I worked swing shifts. I hated the midnight shift because it was very hard for me to adjust to working all night. My teenage years were passing me by. I worked a lot of overtime because I always wanted to save money. I started selling Avon products to supplement my income. A lot of the ladies at the factory were my best customers, and I did very well. After six months of working at Containers Corporation, I was able to save enough money to have a down payment to purchase my very first car. It was a beautiful new canary yellow and black sports car. This was big, and I was very excited about accomplishing this on my own. In this lesson, I learned that hard work pays off and you can get things you want. I continued to save and build up my bank account because the next move was to get my own apartment. When I was nineteen, I met this college educated man who I thought was a dream come true for a girl like me. He was funny, had a great personality, he was educated, good looking, very athletic and, to top it off, he had beautiful teeth. Beautiful teeth and a great smile always got my attention, and he had both. I met him at a picnic. He asked for my number, and he called me right away. Wow, I thought I hit the jackpot! He was all that. He treated me very special, and I really thought the relationship would go somewhere. He was working on his Master's degree when I met him, so he really was not ready for a serious relationship. So I waited and, once he was finished, I let him know I was no longer going to sit back and not be taken seriously. I had shared information about this man with my Aunt Esther. I told her I thought he was seeing other women. She gave me some advice and told me to tell him that if I could not be the table cloth in this relationship, I will not be the napkin. I listened to her and told him what she said. He said he did not want a ready-made family, and that was all I needed to hear. That was the end of it and I never looked back. We both moved on with our lives. That was my first experience of really being hurt by a man who would make me feel some kind of way because I had a child. He even told me no woman of mine would ever work in a factory, and that made me feel even worst about myself. I was only nineteen and it took some time for me to even think about opening my heart to another man. I kept my focus, worked hard, saved money and thought about the dreams I wanted for me and my daughter. As I look back at my life, I realize I had been scared by the things that had been done to me. Words really do hurt and could have a lifelong effect if you do not have GOD in your life to pull you through it. I always felt a certain way each time someone asked me my age because once they knew I had a child, they would figure out I was only fifteen when I had her and would make a big thing about it by verbalizing it loudly. That really hurt, and I started to think about how it happened and all the sacrifices I made to be a good mother as well as not having a regular teenage life and working hard to support her. I was a child raising a child, and I did the best I could with the help of a wonderful mother, sister and family who supported me and helped me raise my daughter. When people do that, they mean to hurt you and make you feel like you are a bad girl. That is far from the truth. I never wanted to tell people my age because I did not want to hear them make me feel humiliated again and again. Trust me when I say I am well past that today. GOD has strengthened me to be able to learn not to allow words like that to bother me because I know who I am, who's I am, and what I am.

Chapter 3

Still a Mom.....A Single Mom – My Twenties
"Rough Seas"

Would you believe that my life would begin at the age of twenty? Not really, but at the time, my daughter was five years old, and I should have been getting ready to build my career. I had worked several part-time jobs and a few side jobs before Container Corporation became my full-time job. I began to think that something needed to change in my life or was I going to end up in the factory where I worked very hard and went home tired every day. Even though the pay was excellent, and it allowed me to save enough to reach my goal of getting my own apartment, I was still living at home with my mother. I knew I needed to make moving my next big goal. Then life happened...

One day after being at the factory for three years, I was walking from the lunch area and a loader moving a large steel crate in the area fell on me and knocked me down. I remember going to the hospital. I was in a lot of pain in my back and neck. I was out on disability for three months. Back in those days, companies had their own doctors that you had to go to. They would really look out for the company's interest and try to get you back to work as soon as possible, and they did. I had developed carpal tunnel, and the company put me on light duty, although I was still in a lot of pain. Here I am 21 years old having these kind of problems and still working at this place. I tried working and the pain did not get any better, so I had to go out on disability again and that lasted three more months. When I returned, I was still not 100%, and it didn't feel like I was ever going to be without pain working at this factory job. They wanted me to consider an operation for carpal tunnel, but I did not want that at my age, so I decided not to have it.

Then after coming back to work the second time, personnel called me in to talk about how I was feeling because I was not willing to get the operation. I let them know that I was still hurting. The doctor had a very nice talk with me. He said, "A nice young lady like yourself, why do you want to stay in a job like this?" This was in my mind when I went down to the personnel department to follow up about the job. I could tell there was concern for me and that they were taking an interest in my case. This was the blessing that day. There was an older lady who worked in that department and was so nice to me. She said, "Dolores, would you be interested in getting out of the factory and working on the office side?" WOW, I thought, my prayers have been answered. I said YES with no hesitation. She told me that there was a job in the laboratory where they tested the products the company made. What an opportunity. All the people on the other side had to have a college degree to work there...or so I thought. How wonderful would that be. My life was about to change. I interviewed for the job and got it right away. The plan was to get me out of the factory, so they gave me a job in the laboratory. Now, I was a Laboratory Technician. A better life had just begun for me, and I was on top of the world.

When I started work in my new position, I met and worked with a very nice lady who became a mentor to me. She trained me on the job and became a great friend in my life. It was really a great experience working with her. She helped me build up my confidence by believing in myself and letting me know that I was doing a great job. Remember, that even though I had not been to college, I had been given a great opportunity with a job that normally required you have a degree. It was very special when I had to go to the other side of the plant where I used to work in the factory. I wore my white laboratory coat that was required, and my co-workers from the factory would call out to me and make me feel so special because I made it out of the factory. It was a big thing back then not having a college degree but being able to advance yourself to that level. I continued making great money, but I was lonely and still living at home.

I became very depressed, never going anywhere but to BINGO. I fell in love with BINGO. That was the only thing I did for myself for pleasure. My sister and I had children who were only eleven days apart, and we would do lots of things together with our children. Every weekend we would go to the zoo, amusement parks, movies, out to eat, and shopping. We had a skating rink in our town, and our kids loved it! That was something we did often. We had an awesome time together raising our children who were cousins but really like sister and brother. It was like we had two kids because my sister helped raise my daughter, and we lived together until they were four years old. My daughter and I really missed my sister and her son when they moved away, but we still did things together until they were in their teens. Later, we both moved into the same apartment complex just ten doors apart from each other. It made life much easier for me when I always worked my other jobs, and we helped to support each other. It was the biggest blessing in my life to have my sister always being there for me and my daughter. It was always about raising my daughter. Never anything left for me. That was the way I looked at life at the time.

My older brother was always concerned about my happiness. He played softball during that time of my life, and it was the big thing in our community. The local men were great athletes. We had a great softball team called the Harper's. I would always go to their games and support him. I was not dating anyone and had really given up. I can still see that day clearly when he said to me, "Dolly, our softball team is playing in Philadelphia today. Come to the game, you might meet someone there." I wanted to go to the game. I wasn't feeling that great about where I was in life with so much pain as a young lady. My outlook on being interested in men was not too high. I was very insecure feeling that I didn't have much to offer anyone having had a child at such a young age. It made me feel like I was bringing

40

baggage to the table that men did not want. The last man in my life told me that he did not want a ready-made family which stuck in my mind. However, I went to the game with my mother. It was that day my heart opened to a new love. I was sitting on the bench watching my brother's softball game, and this gentleman went up to bat. He looked into the stands, and I was watching him. His eyes looked at me, and I could not take my eyes off him. I never knew who won that game. After the game, the visiting team had a party at their local Elks club. The gentleman came up to me and asked if I was going to the party. I looked at my mother and she smiled and said, "Yes, we're going". My eyes lit up and I was gleaming with joy and excitement in my spirit. My mother watched as the gentleman came right over once I got to the party. He was such a gentleman, he was kind, and he had a great sense of humor! He made me laugh and

41

smile, and I was in heaven! He asked me to dance that night. It was love at first sight for me, and it seemed like he felt the same way. We had fun. He got my number and He called me the next day and asked if he could take me to lunch. Of course, I was so excited to go out with him. Everything I thought before meeting him was not so good about men. I was not interested after being hurt and didn't think anyone wanted a ready-made family. I thought that having a child meant that the kind of man I was looking for would not be interested in me. That all changed. This man made me feel good about myself. He made me feel special, and his favorite song to sing to me was "One in a Million You" by Larry Graham. That did it for me. He was a successful business man and entrepreneur. He could sing, he wrote poetry, he was educated, kind, romantic, and funny, and had a great sense of humor. He was an artist, a handyman, an athletic, and he was handsome. He also loved children. I was in Love! What more could a girl ask for? Everything seemed perfectly right. I dated him for about six months, and he came into my life when I was feeling so bad and really turned my whole thinking around. I had hoped for a new future. He cared about my interests, about my dreams, and was always asking me what I wanted to do in life. At the time, I was not happy with my life and where it was heading after being hurt. He gave me a new outlook on life and told me what an amazing woman I was. I never thought of myself to be that special before. He created in me the thought that I was worth having, and that had not been done before. He began to show me the feeling that I had never experienced from a man. My father was not in my life, and I never had a male role model to show me how a man should love a woman. I really began to love this man who helped to create a new me, and it felt so good. I was on top of the world feeling good about our relationship. Sometimes my married girlfriends would say, "I think you love him more than I love my husband." It was that passionate love that you just can't stop, and I believe it lasts a lifetime when you feel that way about someone. I really loved that man. He helped me so much and gave me hope for my future. I learned so much from him loving me and caring for me as a woman at a time in my life when things didn't look good for me.

It was about six months into our relationship, and I thought things were going great when he told me he had something to tell me. I was really scared of what he might say. When we got together, he told me how much he loved me and that he could not go on this way any longer because he did love me enough to tell me the truth. Oh boy, I said, looking sad and confused. He said "Dolly, I'm married. When I met you, I was separated from my wife, and I did not want to tell you because I knew you would not have given me a chance." He was right, that was something my morals would not allow me to do. I was devastated. I went home and cried for days. I was angry and told him that it was over and that I did not to see him again. He also told me that he had only gone back with his wife for the kids, and he did not know how long he could stay because he was not in love with her. He also said that he had waited so long to feel the way he felt when he was with me. "One in a Million You," that is what he tried to convince me of. I did not buy it, and I felt so betrayed by his lie. He continued to contact me and ask to see me, but I refused to be involved with him. I was so hurt and feeling so bad about the situation. I could not believe this was happening to me. Life was just beginning, and things were going so great in my life only to be disappointed again by a man. Even though he made me feel so special, the hurt and pain was unbearable. I was not very forgiving at that time in my life, and that is something I was not proud of. Once you hurt me, I would not forgive you. So when it came to hurting me, I could easily let you go. As I look back in my life, it was best that I was like that because it saved me from any deeper hurt. I moved on and he gave up on me, and that was good for me. I had to focus on my new job and taking care of my daughter. That is what I did for the next couple of years. Then more bad news came.

It was 1982, and we were told that the lab was moving its operations to Chicago in six months. We were given the opportunity to relocate. The company was willing to help us find housing and it sounded great. After just being heartbroken, it seemed like it would be a great move for me. My friend and mentor decided to make the move to Chicago, and she tried to convince me to move there too. Having my daughter and being so close to my family who was my support system, I could not get myself motivated to go. I took the lay off and kept in touch with my friend after she went to Chicago. She ended up staying only one year, and then she came back because she missed her family. I was glad that I did not make that move to Chicago. It was not a place I ever thought I would like to move to anyway, and to make a big move like that was very scary to me.

Being laid off was a new journey for me. I was so used to working and found myself searching for new direction in my life. My younger brother was in college at West

Chester University. I had been exposed to working with educated people and was inspired to find something that could help advance my life. I shared with my brother that I was interested in going to college to become an elementary school teacher and that I needed his help. I was so proud of him and what he had accomplished after going through such a rough time growing up on his own and being the first in our family to attend college. That was huge for our family. He arranged a meeting for me to talk with the Dean of Students who, at the time, was a black man. My brother helped me with all the information and paperwork I needed so I could get enrolled in West Chester University. Then I was hit with another bomb. I was so excited that I could have a chance to go to college and make something of my life. It was really something big for me. There was only one other thing I needed to happen. I wanted to live on campus because I was never a good student in school. Things did not come easy for me, and I was always behind in Reading and English. I was also not a good speller. The man that I had previously fallen in love with had taught me that just because you are not a good speller you still can do anything in life if you work hard at it. During the time we spent together, he knew that I was insecure about not being a good speller so he practiced with me so I could become better. After that experience with him, it helped me to overcome road blocks that kept me from perusing my goals and dreams in life. He was such a great influence in my life, and he helped build my confidence to a level where it needed to be. I believed I could do anything in life. As I look back, I realize that I did not have a personal relationship with GOD like I do know, and I recognized that He puts people in your life for a reason and sometimes only for a season. I thought I was ready but needed my mother again to help raise my daughter. I asked her if I could live on campus because I did not think I could handle raising my daughter and going to college full time. This was during the time my grandmother's health was not good, and my mother had her own worries in caring for her. Although I did understand, it broke my heart. She said she was sorry and not willing raise my daughter while I went to college full time. I felt that going to college is what I needed to be successful but, without her help, I decided not to go. Disappointments are something we all have to face in life, and I know I have had my share of them. The blessing in all of them is being able to get back on track. I'm thankful today as I look back on my life to see how I was able to refocus and move forward after each disappointment. Since I did not get a chance to go to college I thought, okay, I am out of work and have limited clerical skills, "what can I do?" I remembered being a Lab Technician gave me a different kind of skill, but that also required a degree if I wanted to get another job like that. So my next move was to go to OIC and learn how to develop better clerical skills. I went there and completed the course. After that, I went to Kelly Services, a temporary office staffing company, to get some experience. I did that for two years going to different companies, learning new skills and having the greatest time of my life meeting so many different people and building my resume. I worked for a company called SEI that sold stocks and bonds. It was a great company and they really liked my performance. They offered me a chance to go to school to be a broker. I really did not think that was something I wanted to do, so I passed on it. I worked for two years doing temporary work, and it was truly a wonderful experience working at so many different companies. It gave me a great perspective of what types of jobs and companies where out there.

Now I was ready to make the move to a full-time job with benefits because I was paying for my own health benefits. In 1984, I got hired at AMP Products Corporation in Berwyn, PA. I got a good position in the accounting department. I had previous experience working with numbers at SEI and I loved it. I believe that is what helped land the job for me. It was a great year for me. I had a new full-time job making great money with a stable company. I met a new friend, Emily, who lived a couple doors down from me. Emily was an amazing woman. We had so much in common. She too was a single mother of one daughter. We loved to cook and have fun, and we also did a lot of laughing together. It's really special to look back on life and see the wonderful friends you've made and how they brought so much to your life. I learned so much from her. She was very outgoing and very gifted. She was smart and had many talents. She could cook, sew, decorate, and organize events. The girl could do it all. She also loved to travel. I started going places with her because she was always on the go. I will never forget the trip we took to Michigan to see one of her friends. We had the best time traveling together. I really enjoyed my time spent with her and all the things I learned to do with her. We had a couple of years of spending time and doing things together, then she got married and moved away. I really missed her because she was doing things I was dreaming of doing. You never know who you are inspiring in your life. You can be living and spending time with someone and not realize the positive impact you have on them until you look back to see how you got to where you are and the people who were in our life that helped guide, shape and mold you to be the person you have become.

1985 was not a good year. First, my grandmother died on July 29—that was my mother's mother. Then a week later, one of my school mates lost her 8-year-old daughter to Lyme disease. That was the beginning of experiencing the loss of loved ones. I had already lost my dad's mother. She and her two young grandchildren died in a house fire March 1, 1979. The fire was very tragic, and it took a lot out of me. My grandmother was a very special lady who had a caring way of showing her love for you. She gave me the inspiration and the love for cooking. I would watch her in the kitchen while she was cooking and singing at the same time. Joy was in the kitchen while grandmom was cooking and singing. My grandmother was a spiritual woman who walked with the Lord, and she was an awesome cook as well. I loved to go to her house because I knew I was going to get some of her hot cakes that she cooked on the stove in a cast iron pan along with biscuits, collard greens, corn bread, and fried corn. I loved her fried corn. I would watch her and say, "I want to make people happy someday with my cooking". It was a dream I had as a little girl and it came true. Never discourage a child when they have a dream. That is one of my passions—working with children. My favorite thing to ask them is 'what is your dream?' They would always come up with some interesting things. Many kids today do not have dreams because they spend too much time on the phone texting or playing games on the tablet or computer. Free time allows the mind to create a vision.

I spend a lot of quiet time dreaming. I intend to make a movie out of my book, and I want all the things I have fantasized about to play out in that movie. That is a big dream. Are ya listening Oprah, Tyler Perry or any other producer who would like to partner with me?? GOD put it in my spirit so why not believe it could happen? Another dream of mine is to become a Dream Coach. I would love to help others find the fire inside their hearts and dream. That is what keeps my life so exciting and full of possibilities. I believe you have to speak it into existence and allow your faith and imagination with action steps to make it a reality. I do not have a boring life because my mind keeps producing more possibilities of what can happen. I believe I have been given a gift to inspire and help bring dreams out of others.

It's 1986 and my Camaro dies. I realize that after 10 years, it's time to get a new car. The new Chevy Nova had just come out, and I wanted to break out and buy a new car. By that time, I needed something exciting in my life. It was getting boring and that made things a little interesting that year. Two years had passed, and I still wasn't ready for a new relationship. I started to give up hope for the magic feeling I was waiting to happen again. One day while at work there was this African man who was visiting our company. I remember when he came in, he was eyeing me. The next day, he sent me flowers. Then a month later, he had his sister write me a letter from him because he had gone back to Africa. The letter said he wanted to meet me when he returned to Philadelphia, and I agreed. I shared this with my friends, and they thought it would be an interesting encounter...and I needed something

57

interesting in my life, so here I go. I decided to meet this man on City Line Avenue at a hotel/restaurant. He came there with a beautiful African outfit for me, and I could tell he was very nervous. He told me he came to my job and took one look at me and knew I was the one he was to marry. I was very frightened of his desire to marry me without really knowing me. He said he was from Sierra Leone, Africa and his family was very wealthy. That was too much for me. I left that day and thought I would like to get married and have more children someday, but I was sure this wasn't what I wanted at that time. I let him know that this was not possible because I would not consider leaving my country. That was the end of that and I never heard from him again. Now I'm turning thirty and the clock is ticking for marriage and more children. I am really feeling sad about the future of my life because I wanted to be found by the right one by now, but it doesn't seem to be working out as I had hoped. Now my focus is traveling, enjoying my life and sailing along. I'll just keep on living, raising my daughter, spending time with my family and friends, and (ETJ) enjoying the journey.

Here I was enjoying life and still working at AMP Products Company. One Friday night when I was talking on the phone with my sister while watching the news, I heard a report of a man being shot near a restaurant by mistaken identity. I told my sister I had to get off the phone because I knew once I saw the car with his name plate on it, I knew it was the man I was still in love with. I broke down and cried because I could not believe it. He died five days after his birthday. I had been thinking of calling to wish him a happy birthday, but I was still angry with him for bringing a woman to my job and I still could not forgive him. A couple months later, I ran into him at the Music Fair in Berwyn, and he was with a woman. He said hello. A couple of days later he called me and asked to see me, and I said yes. He came by my apartment and told me that he finally left his wife and she was filing for divorce. After seeing him, I knew I still loved him and had not given my heart to any other man. I still felt the love and excitement he would make me feel while in his presence. But we had a serious talk, and he let me know he was not ready to get married again. He tried to convince me that when he was ready again, he would have chosen to marry me. How dare he tell me this after I had waited and was not able to erase those feelings I had for him. He hurt me. One night while I was working at Macy's and was coming down the elevator, I saw him with another woman, and she was beautiful. He saw me look at him and I was sick because he had just come to my apartment a couple days earlier and had a serious talk about how he felt. But once I seen him with that other woman, I was so angry I could no longer work and left early that night. He called me later that evening and I refused to answer the phone. He left a message on the answering machine trying to apologize for bringing her to my workplace. I never forgave him or talked to him anymore. I was done with him. I did not believe he was sincere with what he told me so I had to let go and move on. That was how the relationship ended. A year had passed without any communication, then I heard he died. I had never responded to the message he left on my answering machine asking for forgiveness for the hurt that he caused me. I felt so horrible about that. What lesson did I learn from that? I learned that it was important to forgive others because God forgave us for ALL the wrong that we did. That was the biggest turning point in my life to understand the change I needed in order to have peace and be what God wanted me to be. When we forgive others, it's not for them but for us. My reply is—JESUS has forgiven me, and I must do the same for others. It sets us free indeed. Life is so good when you do not hold things in your heart against others. When I look back at life, I realize how sad it was to be that way. Being angry and mad at others does not give you any joy. Life is too short to let others steal your joy.

After his death, it took a long time for me to recover. I went to work and could hardly make it through the day. When I came home from work, I stayed in my room and cried. My daughter was fifteen at the time and very worried about me because I could not function very well. She really needed me at that point in her life as she too was going through a lot. I was not able to cope with what had happened and how I was not able to forgive or talk to him about it. I would listen to him apologize over and over again on the answering machine and I could not erase the message. GOD allows all different experiences in our lives and, for me, that one was so hard because I never allowed my heart to be open for another man. This time death with the disappointment. It was very different from the other things that I had experienced. My girlfriend and I had planned a vacation to St. Martin two weeks after his death. I did not want to go because I was still mourning. I also had a cracked tooth and couldn't get it fixed before leaving. However, I ended up going on the trip and made the best of it. It was good for me because it helped me stop crying. My daughter would come into my bedroom and say, "Mom, please stop crying". I realize that I am a very sensitive person and crying has always been a healing mechanism as well as great therapy for me. It helps to release the pain and get it out of your system. If you let things fester inside, it harms the body and pain doesn't allow the hurt to heal.

Chapter 4

Mom-preneur…..A Struggle but Living
My Dream – My Thirties

A year has passed and it's 1989. I was about to set sail for my next adventure. My supervisor at AMP Products was leaving and they are looking to replace her. I was next in line for the position, but they did not offer it to me. Instead, they went outside to fill the position. The company did not have blacks in supervisory positions nor did they have any top positions for blacks. I had a white friend that worked in the company who said I'd never get a chance at that job because the controller is prejudice, and my boss was scared of him and will not hire me for that position. In the process, I ended up training three supervisors to be my boss. After training the fourth one, we ended up becoming friends. She said, "I have to quit because you should be supervisor Dolly. I depend on you to do my job…and this not fair". After she quit, I went to my supervisor to tell him what she said because I was also ready to quit at the time. He tried to convince me it wasn't because I was black. I said, "What? You just said it." So I walked out of the office knowing the truth and very upset. I realized I had to make a major decision. My friend asked me to go to lunch with him. He calmed me down and said he had something to tell me. He said, "They're not going to hire any more supervisors because the company is closing in six months and they're going to give us a big severance package". I listened to him. They did not hire anyone else. The company shut down and I got laid off. I was able to get a nice severance package. This was the second job I got laid off from. Here it goes again. Six years and now laid off. This was starting to be a pattern. After the layoff, I reassessed my life. What was I to do now? With no college degree, it was hard to make the kind of salary I was making. Life had been good to me as far as a good paying job. My daughter was sixteen and I was 31. She was going through the teenage years and she was really taking me through some storms. It was a tough time for the both of us. Here I was doing the best I could to raise her and provide for her, she treated me like a sister and not a mother. It really made it hard for me to date or want to have a man in my life. She had her father and they had a great relationship. It was better than ours. That was hard for me too. I was sacrificing everything for her and she honored her father more than me. It was rough seas for us. She was acting out in school, and I was always at the school for one thing or another. During her last year, she missed so much school that I had to pray she would make it through, and God answered my prayers. I felt I raised my daughter to be a respectable young lady with Christian morals, just like I was raised by my mother. I am proud to say she turned out to be a wonderful mother and daughter.

Now I'm 32 and life is sailing along. I'm still laid off and wondering what's next. I was still feeling the loss of someone special who I wanted to spend my life with. Now I had to think and remember all the encouraging conversations we had together about my future. That is what I loved so much about him. He cared about my dreams and he would always ask me what I wanted to do. He said, "Tell me your big dreams." I told him I always wanted to open an ice cream polar or restaurant. He would then ask me what's stopping you from doing it. In my mind I thought I am waiting for someone like you to marry so that I can live my dreams with you. I would answer him by saying I was afraid of failing by myself. I felt I needed a partner. Once he died, I could hear his voice telling me to do it, open your own business, you can do it. This is when I really began to pray more and listen to the voice of GOD. I never did enjoy reading that much. He would encourage me to read more and become better at reading and spelling. I had been selling Avon and they sold lots of different products. They had this book called <u>Walk Tall: Affirmations for People of Color</u> by Carleen Brice. That sounded like something I'd like to read to help me get started on becoming a better reader. It was something positive I could pour into my spirit every day. I started reading it faithfully every day and begun to enjoy the affirmations. That was a great start for me. What was next? Here is where my vision and creativity began. I got this idea from my older brother while attending and watching his many softball games. I went to one of my friends who played softball and asked him if he could help me get some softball teams from other towns to participate in a One Pitch Softball Tournament. He looked at me and said, "You are not going to be able to do that. I don't think you can get enough teams interested in something like that." Softball was big all over in the surrounding towns, and I was looking to offer something different than a regular softball tournament. The One Pitch Tournament sounded exciting to me because you would have only one chance to hit the ball. It was either hit, foul, or strike out, and the games were run in a short amount of time so lots of games could be played in one day. When he said I couldn't do it, a light bulb came on in my head that said, "Yes, you can!" Once someone told me I could not do it, I would have to prove to myself that I could. That was a huge motivator for me. I was so excited to have my first idea on something so big be a success. I went to my home town teams to get them on board. Then I went to other towns in the area to watch their softball games and then invited them with flyers that I had developed to promote this One Pitch Softball Tournament. After all the hard work and getting 16 teams together for my first tournament, I was so proud of what I had accomplished. I always wanted to create something different than anyone else had. So I had the event at Phoenixville's Friendship Field, a local park with a beautiful pavilion and a large kitchen, huge grill, and two softball fields. It was the perfect place to host an event like I wanted to have. I had a DJ with music playing all day, dance contests, and activities for the kids. My brother dressed like Damon Wayans' Homey the Clown from In Living Color and went around swinging a sock with powder in it and tapping the kids and adults on the head saying, "Homey don't play that". They loved it and it was a hit. The food is where I wanted to explore the skill and passion I had for cooking. I always loved cooking as a little girl while watching my grandmother in the kitchen cooking and singing spiritual hymns. I was going to test the waters with my cooking to see how it would turn out with over five hundred people attending this event. My menu was fried chicken & fish dinners with choices of macaroni salad, potato salad, green beans and collard greens. I also had hamburgers, cheeseburgers, hot sausage, hot dogs, snacks and drinks. It was a menu the softball players and fans loved. It would begin at 8:00am and run until 8:00pm. My family and I would look forward to hosting the softball tournament each year. The second year, I created a family investment club called the Winston Connection. It was to benefit family vacations each year. My family was the backbone of everything I did and created .They were a true blessing and I could always count on them. I ended up hosting this event for six years. The softball players and fans looked forward to this event every year. All throughout the years, I would see the local 'Nattle' men who played in the softball league and they would say, "I'm looking forward to that fried chicken, especially those big jumbo fried wings." They really loved that chicken. It was what I became known for in the community. This was the spark I needed to build my confidence for my future in opening up a restaurant. Cooking was my passion as I had been cooking all the holiday meals for my family for over 10 years.

My daughter graduated from high school in 1992. What a relief! It was a rough year but somehow we sailed through it. I went to a graduation luncheon that was hosted by the Phoenixville Area Progressive Club. The club was a black organization that promoted our youth, and the members were leaders in the community who recognized minority graduates at the annual luncheons. My daughter was being recognized that year. One of the club members, Mr. Donald Coppedge, approached me after the luncheon was over. He was well known and respected because of his role as the Executive Director of the YMCA where the luncheons were held. He was a very powerful, knowledgeable and influential black man who was known throughout the community and Chester County. He really didn't know that much about me except that his sister,

Mrs. Debbie P. Mitchell, was my Sunday school teacher and choir director at Bethel Baptist Church where I grew up. Mrs. Debbie wasn't just a mentor to me, but she was also a mentor to all the kids in our church as well as the community. I was very close to Mrs. Debbie and I loved her dearly. She was also a member of the Phoenixville Area Progressive Club and very powerful in the community because of the role she played being on the Phoenixville Hospital's Board of Directors. I first learned or heard, "yes you can!" from Mrs. Debbie. She made every child who connected with her feel they were very special and capable of doing anything, and her motto was "As long as you put God first". I followed her motto because she was the most powerful mentor I had as a young girl with big dreams. Mrs. Debbie and Donald were a powerful sister and brother combo that every child in our community looked up to. Donald stopped me as I was leaving the luncheon that day and asked me what I was doing with my life. At that time, I had been laid off from AMP Products Company for two years and had just landed a job at an insurance company. It was not a place I enjoyed working. I worked in the accounting department with women who were very mean and nasty to me. They would come in on Monday and talk about what they did all weekend, and I was always a very private person who never discussed my personal business. They did not like that about me, so they would say very nasty things about what they would do in their sexual lives. They would say, "Oh no, we have to be careful because Ms. Thing is listening and we don't want to offend her." They would pick on me and talk about me right in front of my face, and I would sit quietly and do my work. That bothered them even more because I would not react to their negative talk against me. It was truly a battle each day to go in. I did not want to tell him that was going on in my work life, so I told him that my dream was to open my own business. His eyes lit up and he said, "tell me more". With passion I shared what I was doing with the softball tournaments and that I felt confident that I could open up my own restaurant someday. After talking with Donald about my dreams and seeing he was really interested in helping me, I thought "Wow", I did not see this coming my way. Here comes another blessing. The following week on Friday, our boss came in 15 minutes before work was over to announce that we were being laid off and to clean out our desks. I said 'PRAISE THE LORD' with a huge grin on my face. The LORD had answered my prayer. These girls had been so mean to me and they were crying about the way the layoff was done. They gave us no notice and they watched us clean out our desks. Those women were so worried about how they were going to move forward without their jobs. The company told us we would be getting a $1,000 severance package. I walked out of there with my head held high and never looked back. I felt sorry for the women because they were so broken and devastated about their future. I had already realized GOD was lining things up for me. My ship was coming in. I said that when I left that company I would start my own business, especially after the way I was treated, and I never wanted to experience that again. Then I got motivated and started my own cleaning business called "Given the Perception". I did not want anyone to perceive me in a negative way just because I was willing to clean their house and that was dirty work. I would interview potential clients and, as they were interviewing me, I was interviewing them to see if I was willing to work for them. Housekeepers are always perceived as people who lack skills and abilities to do anything else. I did not want to be perceived that way because I have much more to offer than just cleaning houses. I did not take any job that was offered to me that I did not feel comfortable doing. I shocked a few people when I let them know this would not be a good fit for me. I ended up with six good clients.

After a few months doing my cleaning business, I read about Black Enterprise hosting an Entrepreneurs' Conference in Washington DC. Me and my traveling friend, Alice, connected with one of her co-workers named Brenda to attend this conference. It was the best decision I ever made. Little did I know this would be the beginning of my true entrepreneurship experience. I was meeting Brenda for the first time. She was a sweet, innocent, Christian lady who we connected with very well. We drove to D.C. in my red Nova. We got there safe and we had the best time of our lives. We met so many entrepreneurs who were successful, knowledgeable and willing to share information of how they got started. They offered two tracks to choose from. The first track was for those who had already been in business and wanted to expand. The second track was for those looking to get in business for the first time. We had been exposed to all these black business owners who came together to learn and share their knowledge. That was powerful. We met some men and boy did we have an adventure. I had two men fighting over me and my friends just kept edging these men on. They thought it was so funny because one of the men was old enough to be my grandfather and the other was my age. It was quite comical. We learned so much and had so much fun. We laughed the whole time. The highlight of the event was going to dinner at a night club in a stretch limousine with two men fighting over me. At the night club, we met a handsome celebrity. One my friends, I will not say who it was, boldly went up and introduced herself to this celebrity. It was off the chain fun and exciting. Dennis Kimbro, an author and a motivational speaker, did an awesome job at the conference and I was very moved by his presentation. One of the things he said that stuck in my mind was "When choosing a business, make sure that you're passionate about what you are doing because for the first two years you may not be profitable. You must also be in top shape—mind, body and soul—because they need to connect to be successful." I brought his book "Think and

Grow Rich: A Black Choice". It was an amazing trip and we have memories that we will never forget. It was life changing for me. It was the beginning of a new chapter in my life. Earl Graves Sr. was also very inspiring with his magazine Black Enterprise and his company. He had a vision of bringing entrepreneurs together to help them develop the art of networking and building your business. This was definitely the platform to do it. I left so motivated and inspired to start my new journey as an entrepreneur. I met so many people and connected to people who had restaurants. I was ready to begin. We got back home. Then the next day my car would not start. The LORD took us down and we got us back safe, even though I drove all the way with no oil in the tank. It was dry as a bone. It was BAD news after all the good stuff that happened. I had a friend who worked for a Chevrolet dealer help me buy that car. I called him and told him that the warranty had just ran out. I was so sad. I ended up getting a new engine for my car. However, I later realized it's who you know because he was able to get the car fixed for nothing. Another BIG Blessing! I started reading the book that I brought at the conference and could not put it down. Remember, I did not like to read at all, but this was something I was interested in, so I finished the book in a couple of days. Something birthed in me that gave me a new perceptive of life. It is our attitude and thinking that mold and develop are minds. We have to train our minds to think different if you want different results. I was ready to begin the process. I started hearing that voice, "You can do it!", and I realized I had to get my mind, body and soul in shape before I could be successful. I began to walk 5 miles 3-4 times a week at Valley Forge Park. I needed something that would get my mind focused on something positive towards fulfilling my dreams. A few months after the trip, I knew the restaurant was my focus and goal. I called Don and met with him as I was now ready to begin the process. That was the beginning of our relationship. He was known to be a great mentor as he had mentored lots of people. At our first meeting, he said he'd like to learn more about my plan. He was straight forward with questions of what my plans were. He is a very serious business man, and he said his time is very valuable and doesn't have time to waste if I wasn't serious about my business plan. His first assignment was for me to come back with a written business plan and he would research several locations for a restaurant. I knew he had many contacts that would help get the ball rolling. I went home and wrote a business plan. A week later, he followed up to say he had someone for me to meet. He didn't mess around. He introduced me to a man who was a millionaire and owned lots of properties. We connected right away. The millionaire shared that he had a property in Pottstown, 20 minutes away from where I lived, that he wanted to show me. We went to visit the location which was a drive-through ice cream parlor/restaurant. This venture was part of my dream, but I had to be honest, I was not impressed with the building or location because of the distance from my home. Since that did not work, Don found another location on the north side of town where I grew up. He found out who owned the building and set up a meeting with the owner. The owner was a little shaky. He was desperate to get someone in the building because he had not been able to keep anyone in the rental space for a long period of time. Don negotiated a good deal, and I was able to get started with the business.

Then I started to realize having no restaurant experience, this would be a big undertaking. I needed to rely on my strong faith in God, and I remembered what those who inspired and mentored me said, "Yes You Can!" I had to clean up the place because the previous tenants left it a mess. During the day, I worked at my cleaning business and at night I was cleaning the restaurant. It took me three months to get the restaurant ready to open. I knew from the softball tournaments I had a following of people who loved my food, and that was the test I needed to convince me it could work. I kept Dennis Kimbro's motto in mind as I was preparing to go into this new journey. Since my daughter did not want to go to college, I used the money that I had saved to start our future.

I was 33 when I opened the doors of Dolly's Place on February 4, 1993. I picked my oldest nephew's birth date to start my business. I opened Thursdays through Sundays. I was still working at my cleaning business to have cash flow that I could count on. At the grand opening, my pastor prayed a blessing over my business and cut the ribbon to begin the ceremony. I had a wide variety of choices on the menu: Fried Fish and Chicken dinners were the popular dishes with sides of Macaroni and Cheese, Potato Salad, Macaroni Salad, String Beans and Collard Greens. We also served Zeps, Fresh Salads, Dolly's Homemade Burgers, a Happy Meal for the kids and more. My signature dish was my custard sweet potato pie. That is what I am still known for. I had lots of customers from inside and outside the community. There were no soul food places in the area at that time. I also had a lot of customers from the hotel that was above the restaurant. The hotel did not have a good reputation, and I did not know that when I moved in. I lived in Phoenixville all my life but was not aware of all the negative things that went on in this hotel. It did not take long to figure this out though. Drug sales and users were a huge population. You name it and it was living in the hotel and they were some of my regular customers. One of my brothers, who lived with me, and a family friend worked at the restaurant. Also Sylvia, a faithful cousin, worked every week for free. My mother was still working at the State Hospital in Coatesville, PA. She would get up at 5:00am every morning and then came to the restaurant to help out. My sister, June, worked every Friday faithfully, and my daughter helped when she was needed. I could always count on her. My whole family would stop by just about every day. It was so beautiful to have my family by my side and supporting me in this way. The first year was awesome. In November of the first year, a house three doors up from the restaurant that went on sale. My cousin Lillie who lived next door to the house said, "Dolly you better get up here right away. They have not put this house on the market yet." So I visited the house and fell in love with it right away. It was beautiful. It had five big bedrooms and a big kitchen, which was a must. That sold me. The owner gave me a great price that I could afford. What a blessing I thought, life was really cruising right along. A year prior to buying my home, I had been offered to buy a Habitat house because I was a single parent. I thank GOD I turned it down and purchased the home that was steps away from my business. Things were going well. At the beginning of the new year, I got a letter in the mail telling me the name of my business 'Dolly's Place' had already been taken in the state of Pennsylvania and I could not use it. I had to come up with a new name for my business. I had a best friend, Jane, who was my childhood friend and we called ourselves, Oprah and Gail. We were on the phone everyday sharing our lives. I told her that I had to come up with a new name and she came up with "Dolly's Dish". I loved it and I renamed my business to Dolly's Dish. I love it much better than Dolly's Place. It had a better ring to it and I could use it in marketing the restaurant. I began marketing and advertising my specials on paper plates ("dish"). The business began to take off with the new name and everyone loved it. I am so thankful to my best friend Jane who gave me the new name. She was dear to me. We shared so much together, and we always had one another's back. I am so grateful for the many friends who have helped me along my journey in life. I owe so much to Jane. Her and her three daughters worked in the restaurant with me. As I look back and think about having a special friend like Jane, I do not know what direction my life could have taken. One thing I can say about all my friends in my path, they all had a positive outlook on life and were always there to support me in all my ventures…and I had quite a few. The favorite line my family and friends would say was, "THERE SHE GOES AGAIN". I kept that line very true to their beliefs in me. GOD was always creating a new vision in my head of some dream I could accomplish. Business was going great the first year. One Friday when my sister June came in, she shared some shocking news. She said she was pregnant. Neither one of us could believe it. She said she and her husband had not planned this…but GOD did. She already had a son and daughter and thought she was done. June was looking to retire early from her job, and I was looking for her to help me with the catering part of my business as things were going so well and I wanted to expand. June worked faithfully every Friday until she had her daughter, Alyssa, in July of 1994. If that was not a shock, wait until you hear this. Not only was June pregnant, five out of my mother's seven children were giving birth to children that year. The family was in disbelief of what was happening in our lives. My mother did not know what to feel, happy or concerned, it was happening all at once. It was an exciting year for the family. They all spent time at the restaurant eating and working every week. It was the meeting place for the family and friends. My accountant, Jon, said I should rename the restaurant to "Dolly's House of Friends" where friendships are made because that is what it felt like most of the time. Most of my customers were family friends, and new customers would become friends of the family. As I reflect on time spent building the business, I could see that the developing of relationships and friendships were made. I met a woman while in the business named Ellen. Ellen came in to the restaurant and began to develop a friendship with me. She had lots of knowledge and experience with catering and began to help me in that part of the business. I was blessed to have her come into my life and share her knowledge. Remember, I had no experience in the restaurant or catering business. My passion was cooking, and I believe that GOD would provide everything and everyone I needed to fulfill my goal. Another person who really shared their knowledge with me was one of my vendors, Mr. C. He was an Italian man who had been in the business for over forty years. He knew all the ins and outs and short cuts you would need in the business. When he would bring me my orders, he would answer all my questions and share anything that would help me. It was not just a delivery order each week, it was a mentoring session for me. Where do you get that kind of help these days? As I look back, I share with you how blessed I was in my life. Yes! GOD IS GOOD! He has been putting great people in my life to guide me along the way. I was never afraid to ask for help when I was not sure about something because I was opened minded and wanted to learn new things. I believe that is why my life is so exciting to me. I always have something new that I am creating or learning. You must prepare your life in ways that help you find your gifts and your passion of what makes you happy and brings you joy. Here we are in 1994 with five new additions to the family—three boys and two girls. It was quite a year. It was a buddle of joy to the family. We all spread our love for the new little ones, and we gave lots of attention to them. My daughter stepped in and helped out quite a bit that year. The business was still moving along, and I was in enjoying my time in my new home. After the second year into the business, the sale of drugs was at a very high level. Drug dealers were getting comfortable outside of my business making sales. It began to become a real problem for me. I had a great relationship with the dealers and they were also my customers. I started to have a talk with them about disrespecting my business, and they would listen for a little bit but then go right back to selling. Consequently, drug users started coming in just to buy a small soft drink for 25¢ so they could get change for their dealers. I did not realize at first why these customers where coming into my store with twenty dollars bills all the time only making a 25¢ purchase. However, it did not take long for me to shut this down. I was not going to allow my business to be a part of something I was totally against. I did not realize what I was witnessing everyday would have a huge effect on my development of compassion that I had for the drug and alcohol addiction I was facing daily with customers I would encounter. I became very caring instead of judging what was happening. I was wondering how and why people were so hooked on drugs and alcohol. I began to develop a closer relationship with the customers I knew were facing hardships. I will never forget a young girl about eighteen years old who was prostituting herself for drugs. She was on crack and said her family had sent her to several rehabs, but she was not able to complete the programs or when she did complete one or two, so would go right back out there again. Her family had given up on her and she was left feeling hopeless. Story after story and crisis after crisis became a weekly segment of my life in the business. I was supposed to be feeding the body and, in return, I became more interested in how I could help their minds. I started putting daily positive quotes in my store right beside the register. When you came in to buy something, you would have to see it. I used it as a conversation piece when people came in or were waiting for their food order. It really started to weigh on me. I finally approached one of the drug dealers and had a heart-to-heart conversation about why they were disrespecting me and my business. He was very honest with me about why. He said that with no education and lack of any decent employment, this was fast money. On a good week, he said you could make up to $3,000. Dealers would come in to buy something and pull out a big wad of cash that I could see. I told him how much it hurt me while I was trying to be an honest business woman refusing to get involved in selling drug paraphernalia. They would always go in to town to buy those items for their mess. I started selling cigarettes, but I had such a problem with people who used drugs wanting to purchase matches that I stopped selling them. My moral belief in doing the right thing was really getting tough on me. Not only were the drugs a problem, I had steps outside of my business to get into the restaurant where kids were hanging out and refused to move when customers were coming in. We would tell them to move and they would say they were waiting for their order. It became a constant battle for me and my staff. I was struggling with these things every day all while I was trying to build a successful business. It really had a negative impact on my business. I remember one day a white male school teacher who was a friend came to my restaurant. After his experience, he thought it was necessary to share it with me. He said that when he came to the restaurant, he was approached by a drug dealer asking him if he needed anything. He was very frightened and did not like the feeling he had. I lost a lot of customers due to the drug dealers, and the restaurant began to get a bad reputation because of them. I really needed to do something about this. I decided to have a conversation with the owner to try to deal with this crisis, but nothing was done.

We are now in 1995. This was a big year where across the county, drugs were a real problem in our neighborhoods. I identified with them greatly because I was struggling with them all the time. This was the year the "Million Man March" was held in Washington, DC. It was an exciting time for both men and women to come together and begin to care about their communities and what was happening to our people. My brother Ken and four of his friends were in the barbershop one day and decided to do something about the problem in our neighborhood. They started a nonprofit organization and called it Phoenixville Area Positive Alternatives (PAPA). My brother shared his brilliant idea with me and I was so excited for him and his friends, but it was for men only. That was okay because I knew my brother would share everything with me and I could give my input to him. My brother Ken and I were blessed with vision as a gift and we were very creative. Together we could make something work. We talked about how when I was successful with my business, we could put a Community Center in Phoenixville. I already had my mind on a building across the street from my restaurant. It was a huge building that had been many different establishments. I had my eye on that building a long time and wanted it for my center someday. One day after Ken stared PAPA, I asked him to come to Richards Lane where there used to be a park for the kids. I told him I wanted to deal with the problem of kids hanging out in front of my restaurant. We went back to the area and witnessed that some men made it a little drinking joint for their pleasure. It was quite disgraceful. They had taken over the park. There wasn't any equipment for the kids, just couches and barbecue pits for cooking and men were hanging out there drinking. This was a borough problem that really needed to be dealt with. It wasn't going to be an easy task, but I knew my brother could take it on. He developed a strategic plan with the PAPA organization to address the problem with the borough. He had a meeting with the Parks and Recreation Department, so he could share his concerns for the kids and the

Community Park that had been neglected by the borough. He was able to get their attention and shame them into doing something about it. It was time to pull the community together for this massive cleanup at Richards Lane Park. Ken pulled it together with over one hundred volunteers who wanted to see this park given back to the kids. There was a gentleman named Mr. Mossy who lived next to the park. He owned a landscaping business and agreed to cut down all the trees. This would have cost the borough over $10,000 for that service, and Ken was able to get it done for free. My brother is amazing when he is passionate about something and will fight for a cause he believes in. I give him credit for the huge undertaking of that project. We are so proud of it today because of all our work and vision and the role others played in making it happen. The park has been named after my little cousin, CJ Saunders, after his death in 1988. PAPA has adopted that park, and we work in great partnership with the Parks and Recreation Department today. Look what the LORD can do when we come together for the common good of the community. I am so thankful for the blessing that the community continues to cherish today for our youth. We are coming to the end of my second year in business and so much has happened in the last couple of years with the new babies, Ken starting PAPA organization, and the cleanup of the park. During that time, PAPA started hosting their board meetings at my restaurant. Although it was for men, I benefitted being a part because of my brother—plus, we were so close, we shared our dreams and future together. I believed in their mission of supporting the youth of Phoenixville, so they would become productive adults through programs that have a positive impact on their self-esteem and development of life skills, and I vowed to support them in any way I could. The vision was for PAPA to be an independent, community-centered innovator of enrichment opportunities for ALL youth and to someday open their own community center in Phoenixville. Life was getting very exciting and busy for me. Then there was another trial. The health inspector came to inspect the restaurant. I got a pretty good report except for the frying I was doing in my restaurant. The law required that I have a ventilating, stainless steel hood put in place within one year or I would no longer be able to fry any foods. That was a huge part of my business and I could not afford to do that. I had to make some serious decisions for my business and my future that could be a big turning point in my life. Donald had been a huge part of my business life in many of the decisions I made so far, so I ran it by him. He suggested that I move on the south side of town to get away from all the problems I faced in this bad location. That was surely a large issue, and it meant starting all over and spending a lot of money to do so. I was established. I was also conveniently located one step away from my home, and I really did not want to move. It was the best thing for me, but I was afraid to make that move, so I made a deal with the owner to work with me and upgrade the restaurant to proper code. I would stay there and rebuild the outside of the restaurant which had been a beautiful bar called Rockies. When I was growing up, it was the happening place in town for adults. It sat up to one hundred people. I thought I could be creative with my catering and add things I wanted to offer to the customers. The owner agreed to the deal and it cost me a big investment of $10,000. I made a mistake went I agreed to this deal because I was already in a contract that was not up yet, and I trusted my landlord to continue to be good for his word. He agreed to keep my rent at a certain rate if I stayed until the contract was up. Things were going to change because I had new bills I never had before like gas and electric and an additional room. That increased my bottom line. With everything I was already going through, I didn't listen to good advice about moving to a new location because I wanted to stay at the present location. In 1995, I got some interesting news. My daughter told me she was pregnant and having a girl. It was exciting, but I wanted a boy. This was something to get excited about—being a grandmother at the age of thirty-eight. I had always wanted another child, but it did not look too promising for me to get married and have more children. My life was full with so much going on, the last thing I was thinking about was a relationship with a man. I had a baby shower for my daughter in January 1996. She got so many beautiful things for her new daughter. I was so excited for her. Then on February 26, 1996 my grandson was born. What a shock to my daughter. The father, my mother and I were at the delivery of my grandson. The doctor said it was a healthy baby boy and my daughter screamed and said she didn't want him because she wanted the girl they told her she was having. I was in heaven because I wanted a boy, and here was my handsome little bundle of joy. His name was Carlas, after his father. I spoiled him, and he was the pride and joy of my life for the next ten years. He got all the love that was missing in my life. I was glad to have someone to love me unconditionally. As I reflect on my life, I can see why I was the way I was about men and never having time to make them first in my life. I had so much going on that I didn't have time to fit them into my life. Yvonne and Carlas did not live with me, but I was able to spend a lot of time with him. 1996 was very interesting. I started creating events that I would host on the other side of the restaurant that seated one hundred people. I purchased a huge fifty-inch TV. I hosted Monday Night Football parties and served Hot Wings. I started Singles Ebony Network for singles to network while having a good time meeting other singles. I celebrated family members' birthday parties in my restaurant. That was my way to give back and show my appreciation for them helping and supporting me. Actually, I loved hosting parties and making people happy. That has been at the core of my soul, pleasing others. Never putting the focus on myself to be happy. I realize I spent my life doing for others never noticing there were others always doing for me. I needed my family and friends to pull me through, and these are the blessings I do not want to forget. You need to take the time to thank people for all they've done for you and how they always supported you. Someone asked me why I wanted to write a book. I said I want share with others in hopes that they may be touched and moved by my experiences. It is a blessing to have something to share with someone. 1996 ended up very busy—with my new grandson, a new addition to my restaurant, hosting all kinds of events and birthday parties, and things were looking good. I was coming back from shopping in Reading PA where I was getting supplies for a catering job when my car gave out. It was a hot summer day and my car was filled with things that needed refrigeration. My sister came and got me and helped me load her car with everything. I was so sad the car was no longer working. We went to a Dodge car dealer that night, and

I saw this burgundy Dodge Caravan. It had my name written all over it. With the great credit I had established, I was able to walk off the lot with my new car. That was another one of my blessings, trusting in GOD to provide what I needed. I was so happy. This was my third new vehicle. I had gotten ten years out of my previous cars. I really needed a van for my business, and that was an awesome opportunity at the right time. The LORD has always been a rock for me. I can't say enough about how amazing he has been. If you just lean on his word when you are down, he will pull you back up. That is something I count on each time I face a new crisis in my life. A problem is something that you cannot fix by yourself. When I have trials, I stop and listen for the voice of GOD to pull me through. You are always experiencing storms in your life. You are either in it or coming out of it. You need the LORD through it all. Sometimes in life we only want to have relationships when we are in it. But I have found that being forgiving, thankful, grateful and humble will keep you from remaining "in" the storms of life.

We are now into the year 1997 and my grandson is turning one year old and we are getting ready for his first birthday. I don't know how, but that year just flew by. Things are getting worst with the drugs, and I was beginning to question myself about the move I did not make. I developed a close relationship with the millionaire who Donald introduced to me. He would often come to my restaurant and eat. He would always encourage me and let me know he would help me if I ever needed it. Remember that building I wanted for a Community Center that was across the street? It was still empty, and I had been waiting to see if it would be listed on the market. I shared this dream and vison I had for the building with the gentlemen who was a millionaire. He always said he would help me if I needed it. Well here was my time to ask. I thought I would never ask anyone with a lot to give a little, and this was a big thing to me, so I asked someone I knew could make it happen. I told him I wanted to purchase the building and open a community center for the kids and the community. He asked me what I would do with it and what I would put in it. He could see what I was doing in my own business, so I gave him my vision and plan of how and what I would do if I was blessed to have the opportunity of owning a community center. He loved the idea and told me that he would look into it and get back to me. He was a man of his word. He came over to my restaurant and gave me the number of the lady who owned it. He said to call this lady and he

would purchase the building for me. He said
I had to do it that night because it was not on
the market, but someone else was looking at
purchasing that building. He had power and
money and I knew he could get her to sell it
to him. This was a night I will never forget.
Then I looked outside, and there was a huge
mess in front of my restaurant. People ran in
saying there is a drug dealer out there with a
gun chasing someone. That night, it was just
my mother and I at the restaurant. Suddenly,
a big man came running in my store. It was
the man that the drug dealer was chasing.
Thank GOD we knew the drug dealer, and he
had enough respect not to come in my store.
The man was shaking and scared for his life.
My mother and I comforted him. He didn't
want us to call the police. We were scared too
and did not know what to do, so I allowed
him to stay in the restaurant until we closed
and until the coast was clear where he could

slip out the back door. I have had several incidents happen where drugs where involved, but this could have turned out worse if I did not risk keeping the young man safe. After that incident, I never seen that young man around the area again. Later, the dealer went to jail for drugs and gun charges and he ended up spending his life in and out of jail. I never found out what happened to the other young man we helped, but as long as he did not come around anymore, that was a blessing for me and my business. The next day, I followed up with the millionaire and had to tell him I didn't get a change to call the lady. He ended up calling her, and she let him know another person called and she sold it to him. That person ended using it for a warehouse. I was sick but knew if you snooze you lose. This was going to be my new community center and I was broken hearted. That was a missed opportunity that hurt me for a long time. I had lots of great dreams for the center. I had to get over that, and I did.

GOD put my mind on a new journey to start a women's ministry. He revealed six names to me to be part of the group. It was group of Christian women who would come together and pray and learn the word of GOD on Monday nights. My business was closed on Mondays and I was open weekends. The leader of the group was Rev. Darlene Barr. The name of the group was" Spiritual Ears". It was a very powerful ministry of women who were sold out to GOD. During this time in my life, I could feel the transformation of what GOD was doing to my heart. The care, the compassion and the love I had developed for people and the community was humbling to my spirit. I wanted to do more than just be a business woman. I wanted to help as a change agent where I would impact the lives of those I had the chance to connect with. The group studied the Bible and grew strong, and the devil tried to get his hands in it, but GOD protected us. Rev. Barr was the only minister in the group at the time, and she was an awesome teacher who could break the word down for you to understand easily. I loved it and I learned a lot from the group. It was a year later when I started thinking that so many of my customers needed prayer and a place they could come to without the intimidation that often comes with going to church. I wanted to provide an opportunity for people to come and share the word of GOD and learn that they could receive CHRIST right here in my restaurant. Then I started a Women's Out Reach Ministry where my customers and anyone else could attend. They could enjoy a meal and someone who'd give a mini sermon on the word of GOD. It was beautiful. The best part of the Spiritual Ears ministry for me was a friend named Karen. She had been classmate and we graduated from high school at the same time. This amazing, talented, beautiful woman of GOD blessed me with the best gift I could have received then. Five of the seven women were single in the group and, when we got together, there would always be a conversation involving men. At the time, I had two customers who were in town for work and were staying at the hotel upstairs. They were a father in-law and son in-law who would come in the restaurant every day to eat dinner. They both liked me, and the ladies knew it and would tease me. I did not like the older man because he was very pushy with me about his feelings for me. The son in-law was a gentleman, very interesting and we had great conversations. He was easy to talk to and, I must say, I enjoyed his flirting a little. It made for a nice day when he came in. He was handsome and had a nice body. I was human. I knew that it would not go anywhere, but the ladies continued to tease me each week. One Monday night, the older gentleman came in to give me a radio for the group. The ladies said I should give it back. I did not want to hurt his feelings, so I kept it. I was not receiving it in the wrong way, and I thought of it as a gift to my restaurant. It was a huge radio, something I did not have. The son-in-law knew his father-in-law liked me and he would tease me about it. It was a crazy time in my life. Getting back to Karen and our talking about men. She said, "You know how when we fall in love with a man and how exciting we feel, and all we want to do is talk about him? Why don't we do that about JESUS when we fall in love with him?" Great question, I thought. Then she read the poem entitled "Be Satisfied with Me" and the tears came running down my face. Then she said,

"I write love letters to JESUS every day, and I let him know how I feel." Well that did it for me. I was waiting for that special man to find me, and I had not yet understood what GOD—the One who gave me life and breath each day—needed from me. So how was I to expect him to send me that man of my dreams? I went home and the very next day I begin to write love letters to JESUS about how I felt. Nineteen years later and I'm still writing. I have such a special personal relationship with GOD that is so powerful, I want to share with all who will listen to how much I love and adore him. He will always be the man I need in my life. I would love to share my life with a man that would understand we love GOD together first, and we would share our love for one another. I had men say to me, "You are like a brick wall and you will not let anyone in." That is not true! You would have to be very special for that to happen and understand my purpose in life and be willing to love and trust me. That is the most important thing in a relationship: communicating your feelings and understanding and trusting in GOD and your relationship. Relationships are key to our lives, and I am very careful of who I let into my life. I do not have a lot of regrets. There is a reason and season for people to pass through our lives. GOD is the reason I hold true to my morals, my character, my family, my friends and my community. It is not all about me. It's about being "Here To Serve" GOD's people.

Some new and interesting things happened in my life in 1997. I had a male customer who would come for lunch a couple times a week. He was a tall handsome gentleman and a business man. He was also kind, very intelligent with a shyness to him, and very attentive to women. I was very taken with his conversations, and we had great ones. He would always eat in, and I always knew what he wanted to order. I would get excited when he came in, although he really never knew it. He was married and that was something I kept in mind, especially after being traumatized by a previous similar relationship where I learned my lesson and vowed never to allow myself to repeat it. I was attracted to him, but I knew he was a gentleman and would not go there. We became closer, and I could tell he was starting to feel something for me because he came more often. I would also catch him watching me. I then felt I needed help, advice on how to handle the situation. I went to my mentor, Donald, and shared what was happening to me. He said I need to start asking him about his wife. He talked about his kids and going fishing with his dad all the time, but the subject of his wife never came up. Donald said to ask him to bring his wife to the restaurant on the weekends since it was different than the normal work days when he'd come for lunch. That was great advice from my mentor who became like a father that I never had. I waited for the next time and the right time when he'd come in again. He knew when it was the best time to come because I always seemed to have time to talk to him then. I took Don's advice and started asking questions about his wife. He was shocked, and it really seemed to catch him off guard. I really saw something different in him that day. He talked about his wife and shared that it was not good. I encouraged him to work things out with her. The problem was that they never did anything together. He always talked about fishing with his dad and that was boring to me. I suggested he try something new with his wife that caused them to do it together as a couple. I told him about a golf trip I took every year with the Black Enterprise Golf and Tennis Challenge. I would come back from the trip all fired up and excited about the experience and what was ahead for my future. I could tell he was interested. After asking the right questions and telling him to bring his wife to the restaurant so I could meet her, it made him stay away for a couple months. I believe I did the right thing for both of us since we were having feelings for one another. Besides, I wasn't willing to share my man with anyone else. I felt if I was not **all** he needed, then he wasn't the man for me. After those couple months had passed, he came back to the restaurant and thanked me for the advice. He said he and his wife were taking golf lessons and that it was helping their marriage tremendously. I was so happy for him and that made me think even more of him as a real man. Communication is the key to knowing and understanding one another's feelings. Talking to and looking at me was not the answer for him. They eventually worked things out, and that was something that made me very proud of him. If he had been single, he definitely would have been my kind of man.

September 22, 1997 was a sad day for our family. My little cousin, C'Jon Edward Saunders was killed in a freak accident in the parking lot of the CAT Pickering Campus in Phoenixville. Several young students were playing around and C'Jon was on top on the car. The driver was going fast over a speed bump and C'Jon fell off the car. He died on the way to hospital. He was fifteen years old. C'Jon was so special to me. He and his sister, Cecelia, both worked in my restaurant. C'Jon loved my grandson, Carlas, so much. Carlas was only one year old when C'Jon worked for me. C'Jon was very tall and loved basketball, and he was also a star athlete. When Carlas would come in the store, C'Jon would pick him up and play with him, it made him laugh hysterically. It was a joy to see the two of them together. C'Jon had the sweetest personality and everyone loved him so much. He was very likeable and easy to work with. I loved having him work at the restaurant because he was comical and made me laugh too whenever I would be around him. So it was not easy to hear the news of his death. His father, Neal, was my favorite cousin and my heart went out for him. I cannot ever remember asking Neal to do something for me and him ever hesitating or saying no. He was always there for me. He had a truck and when I had to move in a snow storm, he came and moved me in my apartment. Later when I moved to my new home, he picked up and moved in every piece of furniture I had. He was my own personal mover. He was the kind of person you did NOT want to see in pain. He was a single father who did an outstanding job raising his two kids. He made so many sacrifices to provide a good, safe and healthy life for his children. One year, he won the Father of the Year Award for his great fathering. He is the kind of person you want in your life. C'Jon's death left everyone in so much pain. I had never been to a home going service with so many people present, especially young people. A plaque marker was erected at Richard's Lane Park that was renamed "C'Jon Park" in honor of his life. That was the park that P.A.P.A. (Phoenixville Area Positive Alternatives) adopted. He will live on in our hearts forever as he touched so many lives.

In early 1998, a friend came in to the restaurant and asked if I could do her a favor. I said sure, how can I help you. She said she wanted to plan a special luncheon for her girlfriends and wanted to know if I would allow her to have it there. This was sounding real good to me as it was right up my alley for the kind of creative things I was doing with new ventures in my restaurant. She said she was going to send out invitations to her friends informing them that it would be a special party for them. That sounded so special to me, so I put together a nice menu with options she could choose from for her friendship luncheon. It turned out to be a beautiful event that I choose to develop into a marketing model by hosting Friendship Luncheons for other women who wanted them too. Of course, I had to have my own Friendship Luncheon to test how it would look and what the outcome would be for others. My luncheon was different from the first one I hosted for my friend. I didn't want to copy hers. I invited thirty of my friends to this awesome event. It was a great way to get them all together. I had twenty-eight ladies show up for the luncheon. My brother, Jay, who loved catering with me, was the server for the day. He was single, handsome, kind, and he also knew how to make a lady feel special. He wooed, waited on, and treated these ladies like they were queens. I had a big variety of food and desserts for them to choose from, and my brother showered them the whole time. There is nothing more exciting than a handsome man to make a woman feel special, and good eating certainly adds flavor to the whole experience. We were having the time of our lives. Something special and unforgettable that did not happen at the first luncheon was the testimonials given about each friend. This was something you don't usually get to do for so many friends and at the same time. I began by asking each friend or family member to come to the front of the room where I was standing, and I would testify what each one meant to me. It was beautiful. For about fifteen years prior to the luncheon, I would always talk to my friend, Betty, about a very dear friend of mine named Jane and how much she meant to me. Betty always wanted to meet Jane since she had heard so many good things about her. After giving personal testimonies about each friend and family member, I saved the best for last...Jane. It was so hard for me because she had been such a dear friend to me and had been through every storm in my life with me. We shared everything together. I was choked up, I could hardy talk. That is a day I will never forget, and I plan to do it again someday because so many years have passed and so many other women have come into my life. The Luncheon ended with wonderful fellowship between the women sharing and bonding how beautiful it felt to be a part of the special day. Additionally, my brother put the icing on the cake for the ladies with his charm. My business then started marketing Friendship Luncheons for other women as a division of my catering business. Each woman who hosted a Friendship Luncheon did something a little different than the others. Women would invite their friends and create their own menu and activities they wanted to have, or I would help them as needed and give suggestions. And if I did not have not enough on my plate, I had to add more. I felt like I was on my own as a black woman entrepreneur in my area. Then I became friends with Delilah. She was a black woman who was very successful in the restaurant business in Philadelphia. She would invite me to events in Philadelphia, but that was too far for me. However, I would go as I felt we needed something like it in the suburbs. Delilah had come to my Friendship Luncheon. She shared how impressed she was and said how blessed I was to have so many supportive friends. I really knew that my blessings were GOD given. What I needed was more friends like Delilah who would be willing to share in the business like she did. She became a wonderful mentor to me, and she gave me sound advice for the restaurant business. I learned about the business when she would invite me, and I would go with her to the different events in Philadelphia, so you know what was next for me. If I see a gap in services, I want to fill that gap. I started an entrepreneurs group called Western Suburban Business Alliance (WSBA). This provided me with other entrepreneurs who could network and share their ideas like they did in Philadelphia.

When I was able, I would continue to attend the Annual Black Enterprise Entrepreneurs Conference they had each year. I looked forward to reconnecting with other successful black entrepreneurs who were living their dreams and finding time to de-stress while conducting business and have pleasure at the same time. I thought it was amazing how this kind of networking could empower you to realize you could reach your goals and stay connected to people who were on the move like you were. Entrepreneurship was one of the most important things I learned in life. You need to surround yourself with people who have the same interests you have. I was never one to drink, smoke or use drugs, although I was often accused of thinking I was better than other people because of choosing not to do things to make me popular to fit in with others. My moto is: Choose Courage, Choose to be Strong, Be Unafraid and Positive, Choose Faith to Start Your Day, and Choose GOD Along Your Way. I would not listen to gossip, and people loved to come in my restaurant to tell me what others were saying negative about me or my business. What kind of person does that? I could share a lot stories about painful things that have been done to me, but what I will tell you instead is that I learned to channel that negativity into positivity. I would listen at first because I was new to all this, then I posted a sign of a little girl with her hand on the side of her face looking so cute. The sign read, "What people say about me is none of my business." When someone would come in and start a conversation that I thought sounded like gossip, I would point to the sign and let them know I was not interested in what others said. It made things uncomfortable for my customers and I may have even lost business because of it, but I was not going to be hurt by what people were saying about me or others. I began to develop the skill of reading people to know what they were going to say and do. The way I could read people and know what they were up was by focusing on looking them straight in the eyes and watching their body language. This was something I learned from my millionaire friend. He told me that he did not have to make contract agreements when he made business deals. He said that all he does is look them straight in the eyes and if they keep moving their eyes, I do not do business with them. It is a skill that I have practiced since then and it has blessed me along my journey. I have shared that skill with lots of people because trust is the key to any relationship. If you do not have trust, it will be impossible to work with them. The one treasure in life is knowing that people can trust you and that's the most valuable asset I hold within my relationships. We are still in 1998 and the drug problems are starting to affect my business financially. When I signed the contract with the landlord for five years, we later agreed that I would invest in the building by making the necessary changes and additions to the restaurant so it would be code compliant. While we had not re-negotiated the contract after I made the changes and additions, the landlord did say he would not raise my rent since the investment increased the value of his property. My landlord was under the impression now that I was making big money once I made the additions, and he thought then he would increase my rent. That was not in my old contract and my five years were over so I was due for new contract. In the new contract, he wanted to increase my rent by an additional $500 more each month. I said no way and that it was too much to support the low income my business was generating each month. I had a lot of things going on, but it did not bring in the cash flow I had anticipated for the projected monthly budget needed. My expenses had increased three times the amount I was paying before the additions. He did not understand or want to. He was having so many problems with the tenants in his hotel along with other properties he owned that were next to the restaurant and hotel. He became disrespectful, nasty and unprofessional to me in so many ways in front of my customers. He would come into the restaurant when I was open and approach me about being late for my rent. Things began to escalate in to a bad relationship. His whole personality changed and he was really acting strange. There was talk in the community about things he was doing. His wife called and would try to get me to tell her what was going on. It was not my business to tell, so I said that I did not know of anything he was doing. At one point, things were so bad for the owners they agreed to pay me to help operate the hotel because the manager was not doing a good job and was stealing money from them. They really tried to offer me a deal to buy the hotel. I tried for about a year to help them clean up the reputation of the hotel. What I learned is that the drug problem was bigger than anything I could handle, and I had enough of trying to run my own business. This was not the kind of business I wanted to be in. Drugs were still a huge problem that police were not doing anything about. It was getting worst in this location and I just begun to be restless about it. There were two brothers that lived across the street that owned and operated a dry cleaning business in the community for over 50 years. They were customers of mine and knew of my situation. They were at retirement age and were ready to sell their business because they were scared for their lives. They had been robbed and beaten a few times and that devastated them after all the years they worked in the community. They had enough and offered me the building for a once in a lifetime price of less than $50,000 although it was worth so much more. It was a huge building and I thought I could renovate and move my business across the street. After researching and finding out that I could not turn a dry cleaning business into a restaurant because of zoning, I was no longer interested in the building. The building had two rental apartments above it and that would have been great income but also a headache. After working with my landlord trying to help operate the hotel, I knew then investments in rental properties were not going to work for me. Back when I was living at home with my mother in 1980, I had a chance to purchase three homes for $17,000. I felt that would

Village". LORD we need each other. We need to come together and recognize the times we are living in. Learning to accept people where they are and helping one another in our community in raising our children is lost. Writing this book is a real cleansing for me to relive where I was in life then and where I am going now. Thoughts I have as I write allow me to share how I feel about the times we are living in today and how we can start a new movement to get people interested in raising our children together again. I feel like I am in and out of time when I am writing, and it feels very healthy for me. Speaking of healthy, I had a lady named Anne Mae come into my restaurant. She worked for the Phoenixville Hospital as a community outreach educator. She was educating me on the health statistics in the black community. I was very interested in what she had to say, and we became friends

141

and I was very connected to the mission of what she wanted to do in the community. She was interested in taking surveys of my black customers and developing an assessment of what was needed in the community for prevention of health education. I was all over that project, so I helped her by allowing my customers to take the survey. I developed a community resource counter and made it visible to my customers as soon as they entered my restaurant. While they were waiting for their orders or eating in, they could educate themselves by reading and taking the survey. The Phoenixville Hospital offered a project outreach program at King Terrace Apartments which was directly across the street. King Terrace was a place where low income seniors and people with disabilities could reside. The program was offered once a week. I started attending each week and encouraged my customers to take

142

part in the program, and they did. My loyal customers went every week. Some of my customers had major health issues like diabetes and high blood pressure. My menu was all fried foods, but because of the health issues people had, I added baked chicken and fish specials promoting healthy eating. That was the birth of my friendship with Anna Mae. I was really going through a tough time in my own life with the business not making the profit it needed. My accountant would tell me I needed to raise my prices, but I felt my customers could not afford it plus I had more kids and teenagers as customers. They wanted fried foods, sandwiches, ice cream and water ice rather than the dinner platters the adults were buying. I had started selling water ice and ice cream and that is what kept my business going financially during the summer months. 1998 was the third year of the PAPA organization providing free services for our youth. They were doing some great things and had lots of support in the community. They now had women board members to spice things up and get more organized administratively. That is what they needed to focus on in building a strong organization. They started with a boys traveling basketball team for ages 16 -18 and traveled all over the surrounding area to compete. Then they realized it was hard to get these young men to stay on track. The next move was to start an afterschool program for elementary students. They started at the Phoenixville Recreation Department (Civic Center) and this helped to bridge and mend the relationship that had once been an issue with conflicts and hurt feelings due to the Richards Lane Park cleanup project. It was great to see that PAPA and the Phoenixville Recreation Department were partnered in a summer basketball league and they still partner in projects today. It is a great partnership where our youth have the benefit of playing in a summer basketball league.

It was during Christmas in 1998 when a light bulb went off in my head. I thought something was missing from the celebration of Christmas. GOD gave me the vision to create a program called PAPA Claus to teach the real meaning of Christmas. Christ was born on Christmas and kids did not even understand the real story of his birthday. We would have PAPA Claus give gifts to the kids while Mrs. Claus would read to them the meaning of Christmas. We invited the children from our PAPA afterschool program and seniors who lived at King Terrace. I had a true love for the senior residents who lived there. They were my regular and faithful customers at the restaurant, and I had developed a great relationship with them while attending the weekly project outreach health program held there. I provided a hot meal for them, and I partnered with Toys for Tots to provide toys for the children in the program. It was truly a blessed time with the kids and the seniors who looked forward to the connection. Every year, they still look forward to having their hot meal from the PAPA organization along with the children and their families.

In 1999, I experienced the roughest seas in my journey. This was the year I knew things were starting to come to an end. I went to get my blood pressure checked at project outreach at King Terrance. My blood pressure was so high they wanted me to go the hospital or to my doctor's office right away while it was still daylight. I was in shock and not prepared to hear that kind of news. My life and business did not allow me to have a day off or get sick because I did it all. Preparing of the daily menu, shopping, cleaning, marketing, and bookkeeping was all catching up to me. I refused to go and get checked, so later that evening my doctor called and said that Anna Mae had called her about my blood pressure. She told her I had refused to go to the hospital. I realized at the time the nurse who saw me that day had a legal obligation to report my case to my doctor if I did not go to hospital. My doctor called me that night and convinced me to come in first thing in the morning, and I did. Thank GOD I went to her office the next day because my blood pressure level was very elevated to where I could have had a stroke. She put me on medicine and gave me some much needed, strong advice about my health. I left the office with a new perspective on life. Now things were serious, and my health became the main issue. When I talked to

GOD about it through prayer, He told me to take a look at my life and where I am headed. I realized that without your health you cannot do anything. My millionaire friend taught me another lesson about being healthy. He said his wife was very sick and had Alzheimer's disease and that if he could exchange all the money he had to buy his wife good health, he would do it. That left a real impression in my mind about money and health. Health was worth more than money could ever buy, and I needed my health to carry me through my life and all the dreams I wanted to live to see. My walk and relationship with GOD had grown deeper, and I was hearing His voice say it's time to refocus and start thinking of importance of my health. *"Here To Live"*

It was now time to face reality that things were not getting any better in my business's location and the drug problem around it. I needed to start looking in a new direction for my life. Children, seniors and community are very important to me, and providing resources to help them in their journey is something I am very passionate about doing. I had been selected to be on the board of the Phoenixville Chamber of Commerce, and I was the first black woman to serve on the board. PAPA had allowed women to join the group, so I was on that board too. Additionally, I was a member of the Phoenixville Kiwanis Club and later asked to be on the Chester County Funds for Women and Girls Allocations Committee. My role was to select grant proposals written for women and girls in Chester County. My health was a huge factor in changing my future by doing something different. It was a hard choice at first because I didn't think I was adequate for most of the "different" tasks and occupations I was taken on and becoming involved with, but I did feel that I had developed necessary skills through entrepreneurship and my exposure to so many learning opportunities. Through many trials and hardships, GOD helped me discover what impact my first real experience of leadership would have on my life. The best education I had was daily putting into practice all my gifts, talents and passion for my community and seeing the work bring glory to GOD. It took guts for me to step out on faith, but I knew that GOD had my back, along with the support of my loving family and friends who were always there. Everyone was always asking me why I wasn't married. I would tell them that I was too busy living life and fulfilling my purpose that I did not have time to worry about what I did not have. I was too busy keeping myself involved with pursuing my dreams. I set the date for closing the doors of Dolly's Dish to be August 14,

1999. It was a sad day. My friend Claire organized a large group of young girls to do a drill team performance at Andre Thornton's Park, and they marched all the way to my restaurant and it really warmed my heart. I will never forget the tears of love that flowed and the joy that filled my heart that day. I closed the doors trusting GOD for His guidance and direction for the next course of my journey as I re-boarded the ship. *Anchors Aweigh Captain!*

I worked part-time on Friday nights at the local BINGO hall where I had a food concession stand. That was definitely not enough income to support me much less pay all my monthly bills. I really was in financial trouble, but I was too ashamed to tell anyone or ask anyone for help. I had depleted my entire savings. I spent everything I had in investments. All my bills were three months behind. I had a mortgage, high car payment, credit card bills, a loan, and back taxes I owed to the IRS. It could not have been any worst for me. It was the lowest point in my life. I had always done well with managing money, but now I could not handle the debit I was in. What was I to do? I was too proud to ask for help and, mentally, I was messed up from the business I felt I had failed in the end. I was dealing with so many issues, and I just wanted to get away from the drug environment. I lost interest in being successful by making money. My heart and soul wanted to bless others and serve GOD'S people. I prayed hard for GOD to send an angel to help me save my home and car from drowning into deep waters, and then a BIG blessing sailed in my direction. My CAPTAIN sent me a visitor, a woman friend who had previously opened doors for me in the community to get on local non-profit organizational boards. She happened to be the person I replaced on the board of the Phoenixville Chamber of Commerce. She was a very wealthy woman who had grown very fond of me. She said, "My husband and I were discussing your situation with having to close the business, and we want to know if there was something we could do to help." I did not want to tell her all the debt I was in, so I only told her about the main ones like mortgage and car payments. She told me to write down all the bills I needed help with. I only wrote the things I felt I would lose if I didn't pay them. I was so thankful for their wanting to help, and I did not want to take advantage of their kindness. I gave her the list, and she said it was not a loan—they only wanted to help me get back on my feet. I hugged her with such gratitude and appreciation. I told her she was an angel sent by GOD, and she told me her husband said I would say that. We laughed and hugged again. Boy was that a big blessing I did not see coming. I was able to breathe because God sent a life preserver to rescue me from drowning in debt. Hallelujah! My home and car were saved because of their generosity. I will always be so thankful and grateful to them and the part they played in helping me move forward in this journey. I had a plan to move to Washington, DC with a good friend named Yvonne. I felt ashamed and I did not want stay around my hometown after closing the business. I was reassessing my life and thought moving would help me get away from some of the problems I was having. I figured I could go to work in the restaurant business there and get back on my feet. Then I got an offer from my friend Delilah who owned restaurants in Philadelphia. She was looking to open a new location in Philadelphia and needed someone to manage it. I spent a day with her checking out the location and what responsibilities I would have. I was so appreciative of the opportunity to get back on my feet and needed a break from all the responsibilities that came with running the restaurant business. I felt all I could handle was being a great waitress and making good tips as the solution to my financial woes. However, the thought of driving to Philadelphia everyday did not sound like something I wanted to do. I was spoiled always being close to where I worked. I did not even drive to work for seven years. She was a wonderful friend to have offered me such an opportunity, but I just wasn't ready for that. I wanted something different in my life.

In January 2000, I was about to embark on a journey I never could have imagined. My friend Regina called me six months after the restaurant closed. She said, "Dolly, I have just the job for you!" Regina worked for a local foundation called Phoenixville Communities Health Foundation. She said that Phoenixville Communities that Care was looking for a Community Mobilizer. We met and she gave me the requirements for the job. As I looked over them, I told her I didn't have the qualifications the job called for which was a college degree, someone with administrative and leadership experience, marketing, great organizational skills, grant writing and experience with fund development. She became a mentor and a dear friend. She shared her vast knowledge of this position and encouraged me to apply for it. We knew each other from the PAPA organization because she had helped get funding for many of their programs. We had established a relationship and friendship, and she was a customer when I had my restaurant as she would occasionally come in for lunch. I shared my vision and my passion of the community work that I was doing at the time with the non-profits I was involved with. I told her I wanted to be more involved with my community and helping people. She said from those previous conversations she thought I was a perfect fit. Part of the interview instructed me to prepare a power point presentation to tell how I would mobilize the Phoenixville community. She convinced me I was already doing what they were asking me to do at my business. I sent my resume which was a difficult task to pull together at the time. But, again, GOD sent angels to help me interview for the job. After the meeting with Regina, I remember how hard I prayed to GOD for direction. I still had my Spiritual Ears friends to lean on as well as my close walk with GOD. I prayed, LORD, show me how and what is needed to prepare this power point presentation. I was intimidated about some of the requirements I did not have, but I was confident about having great people and organizational skills. My gift of vision was evident, and I was a great communicator in connecting with people, and that was a plus for me. I had developed a lot of these skills from owning my own business because I had to "do it all". On-the-job-training was the best education one could ever have, and it paid lots money— the same amount someone would spend to get a college degree. I knew that I would need to work on my computer skills because I lacked good spelling and reading abilities and I felt that could hold me back. I prayed and had others pray for me too. I developed a plan for what I would do as a Community Mobilizer and I was ready for the interview. I remember the day of my interview. I never had bronchitis, but that day I got a really bad case of it and could hardly talk. There was a snow storm, and I thought that they would cancel the interview and reschedule, but they did not. I went to the interview prepared with my power point presentation in all that snow, even though I could hardly to talk and I felt so bad. When I got to the interview, Regina gave me a great pep talk beforehand. The interview was at the foundation where she worked. I needed that pep talk to build my confidence. At the interview, I wowed them with my presentation of how I would mobilize the Phoenixville community. I shared that I had already been mobilizing through my business; meeting leaders in the community, providing resources to families in need and bringing people together. I remembered how my accountant thought I should rename my business to Dolly's House of Friendship where friendship are made. It's what the community began to see in me as a connector for the community and the people. I believe they felt my passion as I gave my presentation. The facilitator of the hiring committee asked if anyone had a question. I thought it was strange, but I remember someone asking, *If I was working with someone who was in social work but not acting in a professional manner, how would I handle that social worker?* I said, being very honest, "I would be willing to approach that person and suggest to them that maybe this wasn't the field they should be in." They looked at me shocked and there were no other questions. I felt good as I left the interview. I knew Anne Mae and Lois, who were on the committee. Lois was a leader in the community and ran a nonprofit that would help families in need. It was very scary with seven people interviewing me for the job, but I felt I had at least two of them voting for me. I really found myself in places that I knew only GOD could bless me, and I had to trust him for every step along the way. About a week later, they called to say I got the job. It would be part-time, twenty hours a week at $20 per hour. That sounded great, but it was not going to cover my monthly expenses. I still had a $500 car payment and my mortgage was over $600. I still had credit cards and back taxes to clear up. All these things were in the back of my mind, but I felt blessed to be given the opportunity to work with the community and help to build it through organizing, connecting and working with children. This was something I prayed to GOD for, and He answered my prayers…again. The interview was during the first week of February, and I was six months shy of celebrating seven years in the business. On February 9, 2000, I attended a home going service for my cousin, Esther Bond-Lowe. An acquaintance, Rev. Thelma

Smith, also attended and needed a ride home. I offered to take her home because I knew her from being on the Chester County Funds for Women & Girls Allocation Committee together, and I would pick her up to go to the meetings. As I drove her home from the service, we had great conversation as I had a soft heart for the elderly. During our conversation, she share shared her wisdom in a humble, quiet nature. She was a beautiful Woman of God who had a gentle spirit you'd want to be around, and she'd make you feel so special as she always referenced GOD as the source to go to for everything. She was a praying woman with a prison ministry in writing letters to give hope to the woman and men for entering back into the community. She invited me into her home and asked me if she could pray for me. I had never been in her home because I would pick her up outside when we go to the Allocation Committee meetings. When I came in, she laid her hands on me and began to pray for me. I felt something that I never experienced before, and I knew something was different about my spirit. I already had a strong heart for the LORD due to the Spiritual Ears Ministry. After the restaurant closed, we no longer met like we did on Mondays and that was a void that needed to be filled for my spiritual growth. Rev. Thelma Smith became my spiritual mother and I loved her like a mother. She took me to meet her sister Linda, who ran a food ministry at the Hutchinson Church in Coatesville, PA. We would go every week to help her. We became so close, and I began reading the Bible a lot more at the time. I was working part-time as a Community Mobilizer, then I got another part-time job at an assistant living residence as a nurse's aide working the midnight shift. Although I was drowning in debt and could not see the light at the end of the tunnel, this is when I connected to my spiritual mother, Rev. Thelma Smith, who took me under her wing and surrounded me with other Christian woman in Coatesville and in her church community. She was a part of the Women Branch Ministries. This experience was different from anything I had ever experienced. These women had a healing ministry. I realized I was still carrying a lot of neck and back pain from previous years of hard work and the incident that happened in my twenties at Container Corporation. I will never forget Louise and Dorothy praying to heal my body, back and neck pain. It was like a miracle happened. GOD had removed the pain and I was healed. I could not believe it. I begin to spend all the time I had with Rev. Smith between working three jobs, volunteering and spending time with my family. I had nothing left to give. When I first started spending time with Rev. Smith, she would always ask to do something that cost money. I would tell her I didn't have any money. She would call me baby and say, "Listen to what is coming out of your mouth. You are telling GOD you do have not have faith to believe that he is going to provide what you need. Change your language so you're thinking can be lined up with GOD's word. He will provide all your needs. Remember the verse in Philippians 4:19 'And my God shall supply all your needs according to His riches in glory by Christ Jesus.'

She said to start saying money is on the way, believe and have faith he is going to do it. I was studying the Bible and learning from an amazing woman of GOD who practiced what she preached. It was a great time growing spiritually through reading, studying and having a role model who was in my life for a reason. When I saw the movie, The War Room, it reminded me of us and our relationship. She was so special to me in a time when I needed someone like that the most. I had also developed a close relationship with her sister Linda. We shared the idea of someday renting a bus and traveling from state to state with groups of women who would line up churches across the United States to visit and connect with and spread the good news. I had a van, so every month we would meet at Linda's house and connect with other ladies in Coatesville to go to Sandy Cove Ministries in Maryland. There would be about three hundred women there from all over the area who came to share in their Christian lives with one another. There were testimonial presentations of women sharing their experience of how and when they were called to the ministry. It was a very powerful experience that taught me a lot about the discernment of spirits. People say one thing and their actions tell the truth about who they really are. When you are placed in a position to see clearly what is real, discerning of spirits help you know when it is not. There are so many ministries who say they believe in GOD, but their actions and the way they live say different. Be careful of who you surround yourself with. I was always careful to select who I allowed in my life. Sometimes GOD put people in my life for the test I needed to experience and learn from. When learning lessons, you should try not to repeat the same mistakes over and over again. I read this book entitled "It's About Time, Getting Control of Your Life" by Ken Smith with the foreword by Larry Burkett. This book changed my whole perception of how I view my time. It was a spiritual book that helps in discovering GOD's plan for your life which is managing your time, overcoming procrastination and making time for your family and yourself. Did I ever need that? It taught me obedience and the key to fulfillment, importance of daily time with GOD, and how important it is to spend quality time with my family. It taught me to get my priorities in order and making a schedule of how to spend my time. It was a wonderful lesson in assessing my life, and time was the one thing I knew I had to deal with. I made a daily schedule, and I was already committed to daily time with GOD with writing LOVE LETTERS to him each morning. Then I added quality time to spend with my family. I love my biological mother dearly, and I had adopted Rev. Thelma Smith as my spiritual mother. GOD placed her in my life to help mentor me in my spiritual growth. I decided I would take both 'mothers' to dinner each week. I made sure I spent time with my grandson who was my pride and joy. I would try to spend quality time with my daughter, but that wasn't easy because we often bumped heads as we didn't always see eye-to-eye. The book changed my life for the good. I realize that time was the one thing I valued, and I was not going to spend it on anything that did not benefit my spiritual growth and bring joy into my life. I was spiritually ready to go into this new job that I viewed as a calling on my life. During the orientation as Community Mobilizer, I can remember being asked if I had any questions. It was really a profound question, and I answered that "I feel this job is a spiritual calling on my life, and my spiritual being is a part of who I am. I cannot separate it from the work I will be doing. Would that be a problem?" I do not think she was ready for that answer to her question. She did not say anything and just looked at me. I felt so strongly about that, and I knew I needed that part of me to feel I did not have to hold back. My prayer life was so strong, and I needed to be vocal about how I felt. God had opened the door, and I was now ready to board the ship for this new journey.

CHAPTER 5:

Health and Wellness...Developing Wisdom
My Forties

This journey on the ship started with my new job on March 1, 2000. This was the year everyone was saying the world was coming to an end, but I realized my life was beginning a new chapter and I was excited to get started. What was I to do next LORD, and how was I going to get started needing help with so many things? I had to write reports for grant funding received from a three-year state grant. My role was to come in and implement programs that had been identified by the Phoenixville (CTC) Community Board Prevention. This was the board that was put in place by all sectors of the community the year before I was hired. Community key leaders and stakeholders did a needs assessment of problem behaviors and issues within the Phoenixville community.

171

They chose programs based on the need. My role as the Community Mobilizer was to implement the program. I had a task in front of me. I had to connect with people on the community board and within the community to get them involved with CTC's model process. The model was a framework of getting the community together to work toward reducing risk factors through the efforts of a youth survey taken every two years by 6th, 8th, 10th and 12th grade students in the school district. The surveys would be assessed every other year working with your community prevention board to assess the results. We would collaborate and work with other partners in the community to educate others of this effort by hosting a Key Leaders Breakfast to share process and update the community with CTC's successes and results of the survey from the data gathered. We would also continue analyzing current issues that need to be addressed or change the focus on current ones. This was a mission from GOD and I knew I could lean on him to strengthen me each day. The Phoenixville Recreation Department provided office space in the upper level for the CTC organization. I remember the day I moved into my office. I quickly learned you had to wear lots of hats when you worked for a nonprofit, and you did not get paid for the hours you invested. I had to transport all the necessary equipment and furniture to my office myself, and that was not easy.

Two gentlemen who worked for the Recreation Department sat and watched me struggle as I transported everything and never even asked if I needed help. I believe they had a problem with me, a black woman, moving into the center. I was not welcomed and that was an uncomfortable feeling. They were not nice and harbored old resentment from when my brother "made so much noise" about them cleaning up Richards Lane Park. I was also mistreated by the teachers in the pre-school center because the office I was taking over used to be their storage room. To say the least, it was not smooth sailing in the beginning. I was faced with a new challenge every day. I would be kind to the staff, but the Director was the only one who made me feel like I was welcome. He and my brother had worked out their differences and had joined in a partnership with the summer basketball league. But the other staff made sure that I felt like I was not part of the center in their presence. I always came to work with a cheerful attitude despite the unfriendly treatment from the staff. When I first started as the Community Mobilizer, I was not in my office that much. I was attending meetings, trainings and connecting with leaders in the

174

community. When I was in the office, I kept focused on what I was there to do. After about six months, things got a little easier. My kindness won over the two gentlemen who previously mistreated me, and they started warming up to me. It was a battle with the women. They just didn't like me know matter what I did or how kind I was to them. One day I came into work and one teacher was talking about me while I was standing in the hall. She did not hear me come up the steps. It was hard listening to someone talking about me, but I wanted to find out what they thought was so bad about me. I confronted her and told her I heard everything she said about me. Her face got so red and she was embarrassed. She wrote a letter of apology saying how sorry she was about what she did. I forgave her, but she always felt that I took her space and it was never a good working relationship with her. Furthermore, my office was right across the hall from the school. I felt I needed to be kind to them no matter how they felt about me. I would speak and move on. You cannot make someone like you; however, respect is something I demanded. I would not let anyone disrespect me.

There was so much work to be done in implementing CTC programs and getting the administrative things that were required. Rev. Thelma Smith knew my unpleasant situation. She was not in the best health and asked me to take her to my job, so she could pray. I brought her there and she prayed and put holy oil on the top of every doorway in the building. Once she prayed she believed in the manifesting of GOD's will to be done. I felt good afterward and believed no weapons formed against me were going to prosper. Hardships had come and gone with GOD as the CAPTAIN of my ship and I continued to sail onward. The most important ship was fellowship with my LORD. That was the connection I needed first—to connect to the spiritual part of me. I developed many relationships, friendships, mentorships, partnerships and sponsorships along this journey. I continued to collaborate and work with others to implement the free programs the community board had identified as risk factors to be addressed for families in the community. I had some tough times with board members that did not think I should be in the role. They did everything they could to make it hard for me. They tried to make me look bad at meetings, always questioning or pointing out what they thought was not correct. I continued to be kind to them as I moved past the hurt and pain of embarrassment they were causing me. By this time, I had the top three strongest women in my community on the CTC Executive Board.

There was Anna Mae, Health Prevention Community Outreach Educator, representing the Phoenixville Hospital; Karen, a Principal in the Phoenixville School District; and Lois, who was a retired community member and founder of Phoenixville Area Community Service, one of the oldest nonprofits in the Phoenixville community. They brought so much knowledge to the CTC board and worked closely with me. There was so much I did not know. I was open to learning and they were awesome teachers to help groom and shape me into a knowledgeable leader in the community. Then there was Dorene. I would often go to workshops to learn skills that I did not have. I went to one that Dave Frees, Estate Planning Attorney, was teaching on "How to Make them Ask". I will never forget this one, and I continue to use what I learned. He taught us to use the word imagine. The example was to imagine how your donation will impact the lives of our afterschool program. This is where the donor would visualize how they could be making a difference in someone's life. We had to find a partner to role play with for this exercise.

I was blessed to have Dorene as my partner. She was a very sweet person who I realized right away was very knowledgeable, and we role played using the word IMAGINE. That was the secret to asking someone for funds, letting the person feel they were already giving in your opening line. I played the role of the person requesting funds, and Dorene was the donor with the funds. She said she would give me the money and that I did a great job. This workshop taught us how to make your pitch in requesting funding for your nonprofit. I had gained some knowledge while serving on several boards: PAPA, Phoenixville Chamber of Commerce and Chester County Funds for

Women and Girls. This was a huge deal for me because it was the frame work to get started on learning how to write grants. Remember, I was not a great writer and spelling and typing were not my strong points. I was in a position where I was always requesting funds to sustain CTC's model process. The workshop was great, and Dorene learned more about CTC and wanted to help any way she could. My ears were always attuned when someone offered to help knowing it was a connection towards getting whatever was needed at the time. Dorene had so many skills that I really felt like she was an angel sent from GOD. Her best skill was writing, and grant proposals came very easy for her and she did not mind helping. She had a heart of gold. We became good friends, and she would come into the office to help teach me how to write reports and said she would write grants pro bono until I was able to do it on my own. It was a little frustrating at first because I didn't catch on too quickly. When I would write a report, it would be more like a story. She said they didn't want stories, just facts, and technical writing is what I needed to get better at. I loved writing letters to JESUS each day, and they consisted of prayers and telling stories that were in my head. I finally caught on and it got easier. What I love about Dorene is that she wanted me to learn all that she was teaching me, even with my insecurity of reading and writing. There was a lot involved with being the Community Mobilizer, and the education and job training along with the angel and mentor the LORD sent my way was a BIG blessing having had no formal college education, which was required for the position. We received funding from Chester County Drug and Alcohol Services each year to do prevention work in our community. I attended every free workshop and educational training I was offered, and what an amazing blessing that was. Some of the areas of educational training I received was social work, health and drug and alcohol prevention. I became well equipped and well educated for the field of work I was doing. I felt like I was on top of the world with all the tools needed to be successful.

AREAS FOR GROWTH AND/OR SELF-CELEBRATION

This part of my life is like a "pie" with eight slices and each slice represents different stages

182

of growth and/or self-celebration. These are the areas in which God gave me mentorship of others some being powerful women in my community that were experts in the area where I needed *Professional Development*. *Relationship Building* was a must enabling me to connect and mobilize the community to come together and work on social change. *Decision Making* was a skill set developed by having the gift of discernment. I thank God for the gift (1 Cor. 12:10) that is a supernatural ability to distinguish between holiness and evil. This is helpful to know when we are analyzing and evaluating what we hear and see in the work we are doing that involves decision making with social work. Equally important is the exercise of this gift in our everyday lives. Others who have the gift of discernment said it's like an internal alarm bell going off. Having good *Communication Skills* is one the most important skills needed. In a leadership role, one must be able to communicate well to build a strong team of people to work together. You must lead by example, motivate by strong work ethics and, at the same time, be capable of *Problem Solving*. People skills are also a must to be a good leader. If you take time to master the skill of body reading and knowing how to work with multiple personalities, you can be a successful leader who has the respect of your co-workers, staff, associates, and community leaders. My role as the Community Mobilizer was to be *Innovative, Creative* and able to multi-task, with *Time Management* as an important aspect of the job as a part-time employee with full time responsibilities including running a non-profit organization with limited funding and being responsible for grant writing, implementing all programs, all administrative tasks as well as facilitating monthly board meetings. This was a major education adjustment for me being a woman entrepreneur who owned her own restaurant. I found my passion of wanting to serve and make a difference in someone's life in my community. I had to find *Work-Life Balance* in my life, and I did so by volunteering and spending time encouraging others and giving a helping hand through ministries at my church. I also spent quality time with family and friends. The most important thing to me was continuing my spiritual growth and relationship with GOD. I experienced smooth sailing through life knowing that the Captain of my ship has always been my LORD and Savior Jesus Christ. Once He becomes your Captain, you never have to worry about rough seas, because He is always there to comfort you and rescue you from drowning.

When you choose to change your attitude of how you will deal with life's challenges, it will help you grow in life. Sinking thinking will not help you. I believe you choose to sink or sail.

You must show up to be your best every single day. We always ask people the question, "How are you doing?" or "What will you accomplish today?" Your drive will lead to enjoyment each day as you focus on your action steps of how you get it done. We are all unique individuals and must find our passion of what makes us smile. Creating something special gives us energy that brings out the best in us. Breaking through barriers and accepting the truth about our lives helps us learn to live in difficult circumstances. It will change your life to do something different. It is called "learning curves".

One of the best things I have ever done to help my dreams and goals become a reality was to write it down. Write a personal commitment statement for a plan that you can apply to your growth in the areas that I have shared in Chapter 5. My personal commitment is that I will always keep GOD as the Captain of my ship. With Him I will sail along life's journey with hope, dreams and love in my heart to allow my learning experiences to be shared and blessed with others. I will always embrace the ability to be open to learn, grow and ever evolving into helping others see the greatness they have within themselves. One of my goals is to be a Dream Coach. I am such a BIG DREAMER and to pour that into others would be the greatest joy of my life—to see others be blessed. I am living in the moment of: Imagine It! Dream It! Do It! Then Enjoy the Journey! Remember, happiness is the key to successfulness. Money does not make you happy, it just allows you to buy the things you want. Things are temporary. Having your mind, body and soul happy is the greatest joy!

Find your true passion. Take actions steps towards your dreams and goals. The best gift you can give a person you love is to believe in them when they have dreams. The will always remember how you made them feel. Being happy is the key to being successful. We all have impact on someone's lives. The more we give, the more we get back has always been the practice I believed in. We live in such dark times now, and others need our light to shine so they will know that there's something greater to look forward to. We will be defined by the choices we make in our lives. Give while you can. I started a movement call (K.I.S.S.) Kindness Is Something Special. It was intended to be a pay-it-forward movement to get people in the community to be kind to one another. Sometimes it only takes a smile, a hug, a touch, or kiss to bless or boost someone's day. I have not given up on the dream, I just need partnership or sponsorship to activate this project into motion. I believe I have been blessed in this work with great vision and creativity. Partnership and/or sponsorship will help make my vision a reality and others will know that dreams and goals really do come true. While some have, and others want, I continue to believe in the scripture that says, "You desire but do not have, so you kill. You covet but you cannot get what you want, so you quarrel and fight. You do not have because you do not ask God." (Luke 24:41) And while they still did not believe it because of joy and amazement, he asked them, 'Do you have anything here to eat?' "Ask and ye shall receive. Ye have not because ye ask not." (Matthew 7:7) "Ask and it will be given to you; seek and you will find;

knock and the door will be opened to you. For everyone who asks receives; the one who seeks finds; and to the one who knocks, the door will be opened."

When planning your journey in life, the best lesson I have practiced was always surrounding myself with people who are POSITIVE and were going PLACES. When they were "going up", I kept my faith knowing the seeds were being planted and GOD was making sure the water was being applied so that I could grow too. Now I am experiencing the fruits of the faith, hope and dreams I have always longed for. Living a life filled with peace, joy and happiness. That is success!

In 2001, my brother was working for the Phoenixville Area School District as a Behavior Specialist. PAPA had started running their afterschool program at Barkley

Elementary School. We had some girls who were really out of control in school. They had lots of behavioral issues that my brother was dealing with, and he was concerned about the direction these girls were headed. I was still on the board with PAPA, so my brother asked me if I could help with a program that would work with these girls on curbing their bad behavior. I thought about when I grew up and what excited me. Double Dutch! I thought I was a Double Dutch queen. So, I developed a Double Dutch program for girls. It was called "PAPA's Little Girls". My daughter had two friends who were college graduates that wanted to give back to the community. Kat, board member and secretary for PAPA had her degree in social work, and that was the perfect fit for the girls. The parent of one of the girls on the team became a coach. The third coach was an educator. All together we had four coaches. We had a perfect match of skills needed to run this program. For two years, we had practice a couple times of a week. The coaches would have group sessions to deal with issues that the girls were facing. The beautiful thing was that the girls were so excited to come to practice and they were faithful, and we rewarded them for it. We showered them by taking them to the movies, field trips, skating and dining out. For years, we had such good times together. The girls were attending Double Dutch tournaments in other states. They even got to go to a World Competition in Sumter, South Carolina, and our fourth grade team got to compete in their division and came in seventh place. That was a great accomplishment for our girls. We ran the program for four years, then it came to an end. Two of the coaches left to pursue their Masters' Degree. It got too hard for me to continue to run the program. It was a great experience and it was all volunteer.

Lessons Learned: When I was the Double Dutch coach for young girls ages 6-18, it was just like the game of life. You cannot wait for the ropes to be perfect before you jump in. You just have to have confidence in yourself to leap in. I always taught the girls that you will need to practice to get good at jumping before you can be a good jumper. If you wait for things to be perfect, you will never begin. Opportunities will be presented, and you will miss the boat if you are not prepared. Life is the same; you must push yourself to start even when it feels like it is so hard to do. That was a very special time in my life in teaching that sport and life lessons to young girls. The challenge was for them to push themselves to be better at something and becoming a successful person in life.

God was also working with me and my health problems. I already had high blood pressure, and now I was diagnosed with diabetes. I did not want to hear that because eating and cooking was my biggest joy in life. I did not want to be told I could not eat whatever I wanted to. I already hated taking medicine and now you want me to take more! I tried to argue with my doctor, but since both my parents were diabetics, I would just have to accept it and deal with it the best I could and take the prescribed medicine to help maintain my health. I still vowed to get off medicines, and GOD inspired me to start a program at my church like the one I used to attend back in my restaurant days called Project Prevention. I already had a great friendship with Anna Mae who worked at the Phoenixville Hospital in community health prevention outreach. I knew the hospital was looking for ways to reach the community in health prevention, so I approached her with the possibility of running a program at our church. I got permission from my pastor and he was excited, because he did not have the greatest health and thought educating the congregation and opening it to the community would be huge for the church. My mentor, Mrs. Debbie Mitchell was on the Phoenixville Hospital board and was very excited about it too. I convinced my doctor, Janet Brown, MD, to be the presenter to kick off the program. Every Monday evening, they would come and provide health prevention education and services to church members and the community. I was so excited because I was going to be the role model showing people how taking care of yourself could help you if you had type 2 diabetes, and I could get off the medicine prescribed for it. I named the program "Aim for Healthy Ways". Monday evenings were best because that was the day we had practice for the Inspirational Choir, and there were about 25 women who sang on the choir. The kick-off was planned for September 11, 2011. It was a day we will never forget because two foreign planes on a suicide mission flew into the twin towers of the World Trade Center. We wanted to cancel the program because of the devastation the world was experiencing, but we decided to move forward and have the program. It was a great program and well attended. A couple months later, we started a program called "Dinner with the Doctor" where doctors would volunteer their time by teaching a specific topic each month. The program continues strong to this day, and it's still being held at Bethel Baptist Church. They recently celebrated seventeen years in partnership with the hospital of providing health prevention education. On that same day, we lost one of the five founding members of PAPA, George Eric Smith, to the tragedy that happened at the World Trade Center where he worked. He was the treasurer. It was also a great loss to our community.

2002 was the last years of State Grant funding, and there were no funds left to continue the CTC organization. I prayed about the direction that the LORD wanted me to go. I had invested too much into this organization and I wasn't about to let it go just like that. I was very passionate about the work I was doing, and all the programs CTC was providing for families in the community. After everything I had learned, I felt I was being put to a big test. I was working with an awesome CTC Executive Board who had also become my mentors. GOD had lined it all up for me to complete the task of sustaining the organization. In 2003, I ended up working for the organization as a volunteer. I was able to collect a little unemployment, but not enough to pay the bills. You know me, I was always working two or three jobs to make ends meet. After much hard work and great teamwork, we were able to pull together and get the funding needed to continue the work of the CTC organization. We began 2004 with all the programs in place. I was able to secure some of the programs with local organizations in partnerships and sponsorships from local businesses. However, my salary was the largest chunk of money that was needed to operate the organization. Then I got a call from Carol, the new Executive Director for Phoenixville Area Community Services (PACS). She reached out to me and asked if I would be interested in working for them doing intakes. She knew I was educated in community resources and thought it would be helpful to have someone who would share that knowledge and was passionate about helping people. That was me. I was always looking for ways to help improve the lives of others. I was

working 20 hours a week for CTC, and only a
couple days a week at my other part-time job
where I worked the midnight shift. I thought I
could swing this too, so I added PACS to my
list of jobs and worked every Tuesday and
Thursday morning for two years. It was such a
great experience for me, and my passion grew
stronger for people in need. I was now
exposed to homelessness, and PACS had a
food pantry to help those who needed it. I
began to pray longer and harder each day for
clients I had and the things they were faced
with in their daily lives. It reminded me of
how blessed I was and how small my problems
were. Everything I had in my life could be
fixed, so I was truly blessed. I was a witness to
many illnesses, the loss of love ones, and
people with aids. Sometimes GOD allows us
to go through many trials and tests, but He
said to count it all joy because when we have
persevered in the trials and stood the tests, we

will receive the crown of life which is a blessing. He blesses us abundantly so that we can be a blessing to someone else.

In January of 2004, Don Edwards was the Borough Manager. He was truly a wonderful man and I am thankful for his hiring me to work for the Phoenixville Recreation Department. He knew the CTC organization was not able to pay my salary for one year. He admired the work I was doing in the community and said that the borough needed someone with my passion, commitment and willingness to work hard and learn new and creative ways of doing things. He created a part-time twenty hour a week position for me on the Phoenixville Recreation Department as a Community Program Superintendent. I would continue working part-time for Phoenixville CTC organization as their Community Mobilizer, and full-time with medical benefits at the Phoenixville Recreation Department, which was part of the Borough. I needed that blessing. I had been paying my own health benefits since 1990 after getting laid off from AMP Products Corporation. I always made sure I had medical benefits because my health was very important to me and I never played around with that. I had to take a cut in salary to work for the Borough, but the benefits out-weighed my salary. This was the beginning of getting my financial life on track. I had them deduct a large amount to put away for savings and learned to live on what I had left afterwards. I remembered what Rev. Thelma Smith taught me, "money is on the way". I didn't have to say I couldn't afford things anymore because I was able to save enough to have whatever I wanted and needed. Life was starting to look up for me. After being with the Borough for a while, a lot of stress was removed from my life.

I stopped some of the other part-time jobs that year and I gave all I had to this new role. Now I was responsible for more programing. I started focusing on gaps in services that the center was not offering. I came up with a summer camp for children. I had the Phoenixville Recreation Department and CTC organization partnership to provide this service. The final cost was $5 a week for six weeks for a total of $30 per child. Bringing the summer camp back to the community was a huge hit. Lots of community members remembered going to camp when they were young and realized it was missed. We had about thirty kids the first year. Then I started a free family night out program, which was offered once a month. This gave families in the community time to bond and share activities with their children while networking with other families. Next was a ladies night out program. We ran a father's workshop, and women were always saying, "Why don't you offer some program for women?" That was enough to keep me busy for a while running six programs and managing the CTC organization. At the end of 2004, my mother was still working doing homecare. A lady she worked for named Nancie had a mother who lived with her named Mabel. One day when my mother was unable to work, she asked me to fill in for her. I fell in love with Mabel. She was a sweet and beautiful woman of GOD. She loved her daughter so much, and she talked so much about how good Nancie was to her all her life. That was so beautiful to hear. Nancie and I soon became close. I hoped my mom would need me to work for her just so I could spend time with Mabel. When you are growing spiritually, you need to surround yourself with others that are growing spiritually as well. Nancie was the Queen of the Afrocentric Red Hatters. You had to be fifty to join, and I was still in my forties, so I qualified to be a "pink hatter". Nancie convinced me to join the group and I was excited because they were all about having good times together. They also had a mission of helping seniors in nursing homes. They would visit the residents, especially during the holidays, singing songs and leaving care packages for them. I had a wonderful experience being with the group, and it gave me the opportunity to spend time with Nancie and her mother. Nancie became a spiritual mentor to me. She helped me in so many areas of my life and I really needed it. I was going through so much on my job with feeling undeserving and unappreciated on top of always being criticized for everything I did and didn't do. Having two strong Women of God who were prayer warriors was a double blessing to help me get through to see the light at the end of what seemed like the darkest tunnel in my life at the time. Nancie and I were really having fun together even while she was taking care of her mother most of the time. Things turned for the worst for her mother. On February 17, 2005, Mabel left this earth to be with the LORD. It was a tough time for Nancie. I tried to be there for her, but it was rough. I had seen enough death in my life and this brought home how important it is to cherish those you love because you never know when they'll be gone forever.

2006 started off a busy year. I was involved in so much. I was very active in the choir at church, I was working with Aim for Healthy Ways program, I was still volunteering with PAPA on several committees in the community, and I was a Pink Hatter. It was starting to wear me out. I had several boarders who I let live with me for two years until they got on their feet. Mrs. Debbie Mitchell, our music director, had cancer and it was really weighing on my mind as she had been my childhood mentor and Sunday school teacher. She would always tell me I can do it, and I believed her. She was so full of energy and someone you would want to be around as she had a spiritual glow all around her. I learned so much from her, personally, spiritually and in business. She was one of a kind. I never met anyone else like her. By the end of 2006, Mrs. Debbie lost her battle with cancer when she died December 12th, and that was a big loss in my life, the whole church, and the community at large. She's someone that cannot be replaced. I would always tell her we needed to bottle her energy and sell it—we'd make a million bucks. She would just laugh, and she had a special way of doing it that no one else could copy and one you'd never forget. She was a Christian woman who represented GOD very well. I can remember being in the choir and feeling like I could not sing too well. At one particular practice, Mrs. Debbie said she had a special song just for me entitled "Rivers of Joy". It was such a beautiful song with the kind if lyrics she felt were perfect for me, and they were because I had been surrounded by so many beautiful people that blessed my life. I received three awards that brought joy to my life. In 2003, I received an award for "Gratitude for Unselfishly Donating Time and Talent to the Greater Phoenixville Community". In 2004, I received an award for "Leadership, Service, Volunteerism, Dedication, and Hard Work to the Community of Phoenixville". In 2005, I received an award "In Recognition and Support of Volunteer Services". In 2006, OIC gave me an award for "Believing and Achieving in a Better Community". I was able to sing the song confidently with joy in my heart.

In 2007, my mind continued creating new ideas and programs to improve and offer the community. I came up with a Ladies Holiday Fashion Show fundraiser to celebrate the holidays. And for the men, I came up with a Phoenixville Evening in Black and White "Males Cooking for You" fundraiser in partnership with CTC and PAPA organizations. The PAPA organization had been honoring a Father of the Year Award at their Annual Father's Day Celebration. They choose the father through an essay contest that was offered to elementary students in the Phoenixville School District. Hundreds of essays were submitted, but only one letter was chosen as the winner. One year, PAPA decided to individually mail the essays to the fathers of those who didn't win the contest. Rather than throw them away, I thought the fathers would enjoy receiving and reading the touching essays that the children wrote about them. They were tear-jerkers, and the fathers loved them. Following that decision, we selected twelve letters and chose a Father of the Month and presented a letter a month at CTC's Family Night Out program held at the Phoenixville Recreation Center. The idea was to highlight the wonderful fathers in the community every month, and everyone loved it. From those twelve, one of them would be chosen Father of the Year. CTC was already offering a program called Foundations of Fatherhood, a free twelve-week program with workshops to help fathers become better fathers. These were wonderful ways to honor fathers. I cannot tell you how many wives, fathers and families benefitted from the program. Today, we have over four hundred fathers who have graduated from the program and after eighteen years offering the program, many are still taking advantage of the benefits.

It was one of my favorite programs to run. It had such a positive effect on the fathers and families.

July 4, 2007, I received word that my cousin Emlin had died. Here we go again. I had been to more home going services then I wanted in the past 5 years of my life. Emiln was sixty-five years old when he died. He was the one who teased me the most about getting married. He would always say, "He cuz, beautiful girl like yourself, why aren't you married yet?" I would always say because I do not want to get married, although that was not the truth, I did want to get married, but it just wasn't happening. No one had found me yet. That was always the topic of conversation between us. He was also one of my top customers in getting people to buy my sweet potato custard pies. Around the holidays, he would get a hundred orders from different people, and he would help deliver them. He really believed in helping market my pies. He had a great heart and I truly miss him.

Chapter 6:

Celebration of Life.....Here to Win – I'm Fifty!

Now we are in the year of 2008. I was asked to be on a panel of seven leaders in the community to speak at the Valley Forge Christian College on what it means to be a good neighbor. I was introduced by Anita Guzman, who later became my spiritual friend and partner. She was a student at the college, and said she had to do research to find out how she would introduce me for the panel discussion. She gave such a beautiful introduction, and I was truly impressed. After the panel discussion, I wanted to meet her to thank her. She said she was glad to finally get the chance to meet me because she heard so many good things about me. She said she was looking for an opportunity for an internship in the Phoenixville community. I felt the spiritual connection with Anita right away. She was truly a woman of GOD, and I could feel her passion of wanting to be involved and helping others. I was very excited to have another student intern. I had a few in the past, but Anita was special. She was an older student who had children and life experiences to go along with her gifts and talents. We met and Anita began her four month internship with me at the Phoenixville Recreation Department. Anita was not shy. She was very curious and asked at lot of questions. She would challenge me by asking why things were the way they were, and I believe that is truly the only way things can change. We developed not only a working relationship but also a GOD-connection. Our passion and love for the LORD became so powerful as we worked together. I started to realize we had the same gifts and talents, and we complimented each other. We developed a

213

special bond and had mutual respect for one another. When two people share great gifts and realize they are here to serve GOD and His people, you learn to get out of the way and let Him guide you. That is exactly what we did. We worked together to develop curriculum for different programs. I ran a yearly summer camp program passed on from a former director and realized it needed some improvement, a revision. Anita and I developed new curriculum for Camp Unforgettable. It was a six-week program with a different theme each week. We thought about how we were affected as young girls and developed another program called Miss LOVE for girls ages 13-15. Then we decided to develop a program for teen boys and called it Mr. COOL. It was a great experience working with Anita. She asked why Hispanic families did not take advantage of the services and programs or come to the Center. She wanted to address this issue, so a part of her internship was to do research and host a meeting with community leaders to ask why it is an issue and how can it be resolved. That project inspired Anita to start her own non-profit called Alianzas de Phoenixville. The organization addresses the needs of the Phoenixville area Latino population and its potential to become an even greater contributor to the community's cultural and economic development. We became really good friends and are still working together on projects and programs to improve the community.

On April 6, 2008, my precious spiritual mother went home to be with the LORD. I was so broken and it hit me really hard. I did not want to talk to anyone. I just wanted to be alone. I could not understand why so many people close to me were dying. It took some time for me to get myself back on track. She had taught me so much and she was always there for me. She understood me better than anyone else and gave me great advice. She would always direct me to the LORD and pray with me about everything. I began to practice what I had learned. People were always telling me I was so strong. I would send people to the LORD just as Rev. Thelma Smith did with me. However, that did not always work because people really just wanted me to give them advice. When it was a personal issue, I would tell then they need to go to the LORD because I didn't want to get involved with their affairs. That has been a hard lesson to learn and practice.

This year I was turning 50. Life is not where I thought it could be. I needed something big, so I prayed to the Lord to give me a vision for my birthday party. The last time I had a birthday celebration, I was 35 and in the restaurant business at Dolly's Dish. I did not drink and didn't want any liquor to be served at my party. I invited 500 people that were on my list because this was going to be big, and I wanted to share it with all the people I had met throughout my life. My friend and mentor, Nancie, wanted to help with the celebration. GOD told me it's not a party but that this will be a celebration of your life in serving Me. That was a clear message to me. He said to have it at my home, and Bethel Baptist Church was my "home" church. Then I went to my pastor to share the vision the LORD had given me. He said it was a great honor to the LORD. That is exactly how I viewed it, but my family did not see it that way. They thought since I love to dance, I should have a party at a place where people could dance. But it was not a party, and I tried to tell them that. I said, "No drinking, just a celebration of my LOVE for the LORD". It was on Saturday, June 28, 2008. It was a perfect day outside. I had a male friend who took me shopping to buy the dress I would wear. It was so special I felt like I was getting married. Then I realized that I was the "Bride of Christ". I wore a long burgundy grown with my hair in a fancy updo. I felt so beautiful. I had my grandson walk me down the isle of the church like a father of the bride would do. The Inspirational Choir of Bethel sang a special selection that told the story of how I felt about GOD. It was a gospel concert. It started at four o'clock, and by five o'clock everyone went downstairs to the Community Hall to enjoy a dinner that I had prepared, for the most part of it. Two Hundred Thirty-Six people came to my celebration, and it was one of my fondest memories that I shared with the people I love. It was the most beautiful celebration, and the LORD blessed me in such a special way. I had carefully thought through how I would seat my guests. The name cards had words under each guests' name that represented how much they have meant to me throughout my life. Words like love, friends, faithful, loyal, blessed, family and so on. They all had something in common with other guests that sat at their table. I had five different large cakes because I did not know which to pick from. I had roast beef, salmon, baked chicken, seasoned rice, parsley potatoes and string bean almandine. It was the most beautiful day of my life. It was like the wedding I never had. I was married to JESUS! To top it all off, my friend Diane and her husband videotaped the whole celebration and were even able to get personal testimonies from many of my guests. Now I have that video to reflect upon for the rest of my life. At the end of the celebration, I let Pastor Coleman know that I wanted to give testimonies of all those who had blessed me throughout my life. He said they're showing up was a testimony and encouraged me to share it in the book I had told him I was going to write. Here I am ten years later writing my book. It's never too late to live out your dreams.

After that great celebration, it was time to turn my energy back to working on projects and programs for the community. Anita and I started the Miss LOVE program and Camp Unforgettable. They were going great and Anita worked at both programs while starting her own nonprofit. 2010 was rough seas for nonprofits as funding became a hardship. PAPA was going through staff changes and things were getting out of control for the organization. I was concerned about the future direction of the organization because my brother changed his focus to something different, and I was left being the senior member of the board and having the most passion for going forward. I was having enough struggles of my own, and I took on problems of several family members who were staying with me at the time. Life was passing me by when it came to relationships, and the clock seemed to have stopped ticking for marriage now that I was fifty years old. It was beginning to be too hard for me to cope with the pressures of life, so I started to give up on marriage being a part of my life too. I knew it was time to start taking care of myself as I needed to get off a lot of the medicine I was taking. I did it before and my goal now was to make it happen again. However, I was carrying problems that belonged to other people, so I began to take out time for myself and read more. That year, I read "40 Days with Jesus, Celebrating His Presence" by Sarah Young, and "Don't Sweat the Small Stuff"....and it's all small stuff...by Richard

Carlson, Ph.D. and co-author of Handbook for the Soul. These were life changing books to me. I really needed to stay focused on myself, but I was so sensitive, and my family would always remind me of that. Because of being that way, I was easily hurt. I always felt others benefited from my being sensitive. That part of me allowed the compassion for others to be revealed. I suffered a lot because of it and caring and helping others get out of their mess didn't help. I remember one day crying to my brother Jay, who always cared about my feelings and understood how I felt. He told me very firmly to stop worrying about other people and think about my own happiness. He said, "You deserve to have someone to love you and make you happy too". It was a moving moment for me, and I finally stopped to listen to what he was saying. I was happy and had joy in my life as it was my passion to serve and help others. But I still wanted someone loving me. I just wasn't open and didn't want to take time to let that happen. My brother knew I had high standards and wouldn't settle for anything less, so from time to time he would screen the different guys I'd date and let me know if they were my type. High on my list was no drinking, smoking or drugs. I liked a nice smile, so beautiful teeth were a must. They must be a gentleman who was kind, had good character and a sense of humor. I wanted them to have everything I needed before I gave up the single life. Single life wasn't easy, and I had been single a long time. However, I feel like I made the best of what GOD gave me. I made good choices and I believe I had taken the right path, so I was proud of what I had accomplished in life. My brother helped me to open my eyes and focus on myself more.

I believe 2011 was one of the worst years of my life. Everything that could happen did happen. I was trying to focus on me when everything broke out. I had started my business making Dolly's Dish Custard Sweet Potato Pies. My customers would continue ordering them even after I had closed my restaurant. I knew I did not want to go back into the restaurant business, but I would be willing to make the pies only. I renewed my business license and began selling my pies at the Phoenixville Farmer's Market. Things were going so well, I started researching the opportunity of selling my pies in the Whole Foods Market. Several businesses at the Farmer's Market were already selling their products in the Whole Foods Market. They said they would love to help me do the same thing because it was a good market to be in, and there wouldn't be much competition for me. But my truly big dream was that I had developed a concept for my pie that was not on the market, and my brother, who worked in the food industry over 40 years, let me know it was a million dollar idea. I am still waiting on the opportunity for a company like a Sara Lee, Mrs. Smith or any other baking company who would be interested in partnering with me. Also, one of my very faithful customers, Kevin Kelly from Downingtown said, "Girl, Patty LaBelle aint got nothing on you." I had so many things going on that year. I remember going on vacation to the Black Enterprise Golf and Tennis Challenge in September during the Labor Day holiday. I was always fired up after that vacation after meeting so many successful people who were on the move of fulfilling their goals, and that is what I was modeling my life to be...successful, enjoying life, traveling, and being surrounded with positivity. When I got home, I needed my mother to move back into her own house because things had gotten tough, and we needed our space as women. My brother and my grandson were still living with me, and I remembered what my brother was telling me about focusing on myself and my happiness. I had enough and said it is time for me to be by myself. I had both of them move out of my house during the Thanksgiving season, so I could focus on baking my pies for the holidays. I would always take about ten days of vacation during that time, and I had a lot to deal with that year. PAPA had lost all their employees due to the downfall of the economy and bad management. With my brother gone, I was left with the task of holding everything together. My pie business was doing well and moving in the right direction, but it was requiring a lot of my time. PAPA was falling apart, and I was the only one who not only understood but helped nurture and develop my brother, Ken's vision for it. I also had a love and passion for the organization. With the work of CTC and the Phoenixville Recreation Department, as well as my church obligations, I realized I needed to find balance in my life. I was going out of mind trying to pull it all together. On top of everything else in my life, there was the Annual Father's Day Celebration coming up in June, the summer basketball league, and the SAFE summer camp enrichment program that I would organize and run for PAPA. I felt the ship was about to sink and I was going to drown. I cried every day. I leaned on GOD for direction and prayed to Him to send some help, and He did! My niece, Alexis had just got laid off from her job, and I needed her assistance. I asked her and my other niece, Cecelia, to help with organizing the Annual Father's Day Celebration. They agreed to help that year and did a fabulous job. I was impressed with

227

Alexis's willingness to help out with PAPA. She had grown up participating in the programs PAPA offered, and that made it easy for her to be a part and help. She knew I was in deep waters and needed her to help with keeping the organization afloat. She agreed to help in the office and wherever else I needed her. I was trying to keep the board together and my pie business as well. I realized it was too much for me and concluded that I had to give up something or I would lose my mind. I had been working eighty hours a week. I felt so weak I knew I would get sick if I kept it up. I decided to stop my pie business and focus on PAPA. I knew I could come back to fulfill my big dreams of the business concept of my pie someday. The programs PAPA offered were very much needed for the children and the community. I knew if I let it go, there would be a big loss and I could not bear to see that happen. I went back to the board members feeling confident they would help. I reached out to Theresa who helped with bookkeeping. Then I went back to Rev. Greg Thornton who had been an original board member and once the President and asked him to get back on board. He agreed. Next, I went to Bernard, our church treasurer, because I needed his expertise. He also agreed to help save the organization. I still had Amber, Rahim and Mike. Mike was President of the board. At that time, there was a member who was trying hard to get me off the board. They felt I had too much power, but all I was trying to do was make the right decisions with the right people who had the history and would step up to do what was needed to save the organization. We all pulled together, and Alexis began taking huge steps in learning how to write grants and do whatever was needed to keep the programs and organization running. It was not an easy task for any of us. I mentored Alexis, and I even got my friend Anita to come on board and help for a couple of years. We saved the organization and celebrated our 23rd year of service in and to the community. We are really doing well, and it is all thanks to everyone who helped. The Community Coalition played a major role in saving the organization along with the Phoenixville School District, the Phoenixville Community Health Foundation, the Phoenixville Community Education Foundation, and all the members of the board. I must also give thanks to the community businesses that supported our programs for the youth and families over the years. I never looked back to say it was not the right choice to keep the organization going. I have not given up on my dream of marketing my pies someday. Timing is everything, and it was not yet the time for the pie business. I took some time off for vacation in November after the Thanksgiving holiday, then I went back to work. There was this basketball team of young men ages 19 to 22 practicing in the gym, and I realized a few of them were the young men who had moved two doors down from my home. They had made an agreement to have practice five days a week Monday through Friday at the Recreation Center. Things were pretty crazy at the center with all this going on. One day, I was asked by a coach if I had met the head coach of the team, and I said no. Then I was introduced to him and he smiled, and I lost my mind. I had been waiting for someone to smile at me and make me feel like I was a woman again, and he did it for me. I never even noticed him for the two weeks he was there every day because I was so occupied with PAPA and everything that was going on in my life. I just kept working and going on about my business. I had not seen anyone in a long time who could get my attention and keep it like he did. He was a shy guy and I was shy too. We were afraid to talk to each other. His smile made me feel like he knew what I was thinking, although neither one of us said how we felt. He finally got the nerve to start talking to me. He would come in the office and chat and not really say anything that meant he was interested. My heart was pumping, and I was very nervous when he came in. I had not felt like that in a long time. This went on for about three months. Then one day he told me he was moving and my heart sank. I thought, why was he leaving? We haven't even started anything yet. Well, he moved. Then I felt happy because I could stop dreaming about something that was never going to get started. He was gone for about a month when he reached out to me. I was so happy. He moved because he was looking for work, and he felt he had a better chance in the south. I knew he was not happy with his life not having the job of his dreams. He also had family problems that he had shared with me. I continued to pray for his happiness and to find the job of his dreams. After some time passed, he finally got it together. I thought he might be ready for a relationship once he had it together. Little did I know he had found someone and said he was very happy with them. It crushed me, and I felt rejected, but I had accepted his decision that he was not interested. Once I knew he had someone, I closed my heart and began to focus on what I did best...creating and dreaming about things that made me happy. It was 2012, and I needed to rethink my life and what path and direction GOD was taking me in now. I wanted to shut down from everyone and everything, so I took a vacation. When I returned, I would go to work, come home, watch no TV, and it would just be me and GOD in prayer. I created Spiritual Space to renew my mind, body and soul. This shift was the beginning of my spiritual journey. I started to realize that I no longer needed to look to others for advice on what path I was taking or what my thoughts and dreams were. Then I asked myself questions like what could I start to live without in my life? What was most important to me? What really matters? Start living with God as the center of my life. Boundaries were something I had to re-establish.

I thought about my whole life and what had happened to me. I cried everyday thinking of all the hurt and pain I had gone through with rape, family, co-workers, friends and how I had loss so many people in my life. PAIN stood for Prayers Allow Individuals New Hope, and that is what I needed in my life. I had a real cleansing of the mind, body and soul. GOD was working on a new me. HE renewed my heart and mind and gave me a new outlook on how I was to move forward in life. I kept to myself for three months without connecting to anyone. I only wanted to hear from the LORD. I would go to work and keep busy while I kept to myself. One day I asked GOD why I was here. He said to spell out my last name and I did...W I N S TO N. Then He told me to say the first three letters...W I N. He said, "You're HERE TO WIN, now trademark that slogan." I tried to get a website with the name, but it was taken. Then as I began to think of the slogan, I thought Wow. What about just "Here to _____". Anything you put in that blank is powerful. Here to Live, Love, Learn and Serve. They are all powerful. Let me just trademark the "Here to _____". Then I created a business with the dream of HERE TO WIN, the new big phrase the world would embrace, and I would use it in the sports world with the hope of connecting or partnering with a company like

Nike. Then He gave me a vision for my own cheerleading chant to be used in the sports world and by fans. I wrote the lyrics and produced a video of a cheerleading chant, then I recorded and copyrighted it. I believed it was going to be big and go viral. I launched my cheerleading contest on Facebook, after launching my new business, Here to Apparel, LLC. I started Here to Connect by being disappointed in starting my company Here to Apparel. The company was launched in September 2014 with a vision from GOD to trademark a slogan "Here To Win" along with Here To _____. After one month into the launch of my business, I realized that a big well known company was using my slogan on young children's t-shirts. I knew I had the trademark seal for my slogan, so I began to pursue legal advice for what to do. Then I realized I needed to put my trust in GOD for His wise and best advice. After painfully discovering that life is not always fair even when you do everything the right way, you can still be disappointed. In following GOD's direction, HE asked me what my purpose was. I said that living a purposeful life means that I am "Here to Serve" and that is my true love, serving others. Then I asked myself what was my passion and gift from GOD. The answer is connecting people to people and services, and empowering women and girls. That is what I spent most of my life doing. Some of the programs I developed and ran were PAPA's Girls Double Dutch Program, Western Suburban Business Alliance, Spiritual Ears, Ladies Night Out, and Miss Love Program. Then GOD planted the seed for the vision of the Here To Connect Movement in 2016. I really got off track worrying about who was using my slogan when I should have been focusing on how to run my business. It was a slow process. I had an online store, and my business was set up to do fundraisers for schools, churches and business websites to sell and have direct marketing at my own pace. My plan was to retire at sixty-two, and building my company was on hold. Things did not go as planned, and the business didn't do so well the first year. However, that did not stop me from going forward. I said, "Ok GOD, what's next?" If I have to fill in the blank in Here To _____, what can I focus on now that Here To Win was not taking off like I had planned?

I prayed about my gifts and talents and realized that what I enjoyed most was connecting to people and helping people. I thought of how blessed I was to have so many women in my life who had mentored me, and I wanted to give back to other women. I went to my office at home and looked through all my files because I always kept every flyer or program I ever created. I looked to see how many women and girl programs I created. Then the light bulb went off. It is Here To Connect with Women and Girls. Connect is what I did best and loved it. I remembered how I started the Friendship Luncheons for women in the restaurant and decided to restart them with the plan and purpose for getting women and girls together. I prayed about coming up with a mission and strategy of how I would connect the women and girls. I developed the Here To Connect Movement, and the mission is to connect women and girls in an accountable partnership, and to engage in physical or social activity for one hour each week to promote a healthy life and positive relationship. I was asking women to join the Movement by finding an accountable partner, spreading the word, hosting a Friendship Luncheon, commit to an activity and then get connected! That is what I was

239

able to develop into a movement that I hosted at my first Friendship Luncheon on August 27, 2016. Eileen and I connected at that first luncheon. We agreed that we would like to become accountable partners and spend one hour each week focusing on our goals while bonding in our friendship. I turned my focus on my passion for what I loved instead of my business Here To Apparel. Eileen and I began to meet each week and it was so powerful. We wrote our goals and we knew clearly that GOD had ordained our friendship and connection. We lived in the same town and knew each other, and her son and my grandson were best friends in school. That was our connection before the Here to Connect Women & Girls Luncheon. We could hardly wait to get together each week to share our goals, dreams and action plan for what we wanted to happen between us. We began working as a team to accomplish what we both wanted and how we could put our empowering women together. My goal was connecting women in accountable partnerships to bond and help each other, and Eileen's was to empower women to succeed. It was a perfect match. I learned from Linda Clemens who hosts women entrepreneur conferences what the word "together" means...To Get Her. So true. Together we wanted to get her and to empower her to succeed in life and to have someone to pull along with you. That was the concept I was building. We needed to have a support system in place when we are accomplishing our goals and dreams in life. Eileen just happened to be a life coach, and she got her training from John Maxwell, one of the best motivational speakers out there and a #1 best-selling author. I was blessed to have Eileen as my accountable partner. She was so willing to help me with strategies she learned, and I was able to help her host Empower To Succeed workshops in our community of Phoenixville. It was a win-win for both of us. We brought so much knowledge to the table to share and help each other. It was a year later, and we had surpassed all our goals and developed new ones along the way towards working together. We now had a close bond and friendship and will be releasing our books together in 2018. That is the kind of powerful testimony that I want other women to share after they have spent an hour a week together for one year. Time is one of the most precious assets that we have to give, and when you do, it can have a powerful effect on the other person. I have adopted this quote, "When we bond with others is when we improve our quality of life." That is a true fact of life. Try it, you will like it, and you will see the goodness it has for the soul!

In May 2015, I met my new friend Cheryl at the Black Enterprise Entrepreneur Conference in Atlanta, Georgia. We both attended the conference by ourselves, and I learned that attending by yourself makes it much easier to connect with others. That is when you are at your best to use your social skills to engage in conversations. It also makes you more approachable. Once I met Cheryl, we became best of friends from the moment we connected. Her spirit and personality were so much like mine, and we really understood that about each other. She loves all people and loves to talk, and that was so much my personality. We had a great time together and vowed to stay connected once we went back to our homes. I have been blessed in so many ways because of Cheryl. She is a woman of GOD, a motivational speaker and life coach, and a woman with a heart of gold. She has mentored, coached, and blessed my life with experiences she has shared that have enhanced my life in the entrepreneurial world, and I am so grateful for her. We are both entrepreneurs and empowering others to do the same. She is unselfish and so willing to help others to have what she has. I am so proud to find these kinds of women in my life to help mold and shape the life style that is pleasing to GOD first and then to each other. I am blessed to be surrounded by so many angels that GOD has placed in my life. That is key, not how many possessions you acquire. All the money in the world cannot bring happiness and joy in your life. My future to gain friendships while connecting and helping others is very important to me. It maintains the joy that keeps hope alive for the very best that life has to offer.

In August 2016, I started the first Friendship Luncheon. It was so beautiful. I catered a healthy salad buffet. Every kind of salad you could think of was on the buffet. We played games and shared and connected with other women, and I was encouraged to move forward with it. This was something women could get excited about, spending time together and supporting each other. I hosted three Friendship Luncheons in my first year. Then in 2017, God gave me a new direction for the Women's Movement. In January, I would host a Spiritual Luncheon. It was to encourage and empower women to start with a fresh spirit to be renewed, recharged and revived. Then in March, it was time to honor women in our community. March is National Women's History Month, and I wanted to honor extraordinary achievements of women in our community. My mind was always going, creating something new. Back in 2011, I came up with the idea to host an Entrepreneurial Expo in Phoenixville, and I called it The

Phoenixville Area Entrepreneur's Expo. Although 2011 was a crazy year, it was something I wanted to host annually. It was a year that I will never forget with all the hardships and everything I had on my plate. The pie business, PAPA in transition and then the big plans of a huge undertaking of an Entrepreneur's Expo that year. The expo was a great success. I was able to honor a few women and give awards in three different categories. I presented the following awards to the honorees: Entrepreneur of the Year, Most Charitable Entrepreneur, and Unsung Hero Award. State Senator Andy Dinniman was the Keynote Speaker, and House of Representative, Warren Kampf, was a presenter at the expo. Other presenters were from Freedom Foundation's Youth Entrepreneur Program. I had an awesome panel of entrepreneurs, gospel singers, entertainment, and a contest for the kids.

Although I wanted to have this event every year, I learned that everything happens in GOD's time not ours. In October 2017, the Women's Entrepreneur and Women Veterans Expo was birthed. This was another big accomplishment I was proud of. It had given me the chance to focus on my mission of empowering women and bringing them together. These events gave women the unique opportunity of connecting with those from different professional sectors to educate, share information, and inspire women of all ages to become successful business owners. I wanted to ignite their excitement about entrepreneurship and the rewards of business ownership. The events also provided an environment for women entrepreneurs to promote their products and/or services. They would be able develop new customers and gain exposure for their business, as well as learn, expand and network with other businesses. I was coordinating the event to celebrate diversity within our community and the surrounding areas. This brought together women entrepreneurs, performers and a variety of exhibitors offering information and goods to sell. State Rep. Warren Kampf presented the "Women's Entrepreneur of the Year Award" to Gail Warner, an amazing local business woman and owner of Bridge Street Chocolates in Phoenixville, PA. She had no idea she was getting the award, so it was a surprise. She was asked to be a part of the Women's Entrepreneur's Panel of discussion. After the discussion, State Rep. Warren Kampf called her to the podium so he could present her with the award. Then, State Senator Andy Dinniman, along with representatives from Congressman Ryan Costello's office, the Chester County Commissioner's office, and the Mayor of Phoenixville all presented her with declarations of her accomplishments. I will never forget that beautiful moment. I was so proud to be a part of this momentous occasion of highlighting a successful and deserving woman in our community. These are the kind of things that make me happy to do something special for others. Gail was so appreciative of everything, and this occasion has since united us in friendship. That is what life is all about, being a shining light for JESUS for others to see. This year, the Phoenixville Social Concerns Committee honored me at their Annual Community Prayer Breakfast and presented me with the Rev. Dr. Martin Luther King, Jr. Humanitarian Award. This blew me away. I did not expect anything like that. I was so shocked to be given such a prestigious award. I had received other awards in my life, but none like this and it meant so much to me to receive it. What made it even more special was that Donald Coppedge, my mentor and father figure, presented the award to me. He gave me two minutes to make a speech, and he was the kind of person who would stop you if you went over time. He did not play when it came to public speaking. I was under pressure to say everything I felt I needed to say. My heart was pounding so fast, and I wanted to thank everyone who was a part of helping mold me to the woman I am today. Donald always said that the one thing he wanted for mentoring me was that I give back and help someone else. I let him know that I always kept that in my heart, and I appreciated all he did for me. After getting that award, GOD told me there was much more to do and that He would be right there to help me do it. More is what I am ready for. Oh boy, I thought, what would my mind be thinking up next? Abdul Kelly was the keynote speaker for the breakfast. He was such a dynamic speaker, and we connected after the breakfast. His message was "Coming Together, Embracing Diversity". I let him know how proud I was of him. He was a young black man and a powerful motivational speaker who stood strong in front of the large diversity of the faith community and addressed issues that were very uncomfortable for some in attendance. He poured out his heart about taking action against systematic racism. He and I connected a day later, and I followed up with him right away. He asked if I would help him in his mission. Oh boy, that is all I need when I am passionate about something, so I said yes. I shared with him that I wanted to be a mentor and a source in helping him with his mission. Two months later, while he was living in Virginia, we started communicating by emails and phone calls. After that short period of time, we came up with a movement called "Here To Unite". The goal of the movement was grassroots dedicated to coming together, embracing diversity and creating change accomplished by taking action against systematic racism in our communities. We developed a tagline of "Coming Together, Connecting People, and Communicating with one another in order to Embrace Diversity". We were charged up and ready to make changes in our community. Abdul is an awesome young man who is finishing his Master's program, and we are looking forward to working together in our movement to make changes in the communities and the world. This year has been explosive for me to all that GOD has done in my life and what He has in store. I did a lot of traveling to women's conferences and learned a great deal that helped with my physical and spiritual growth. My passion is to empower as many women as possible, so I decided next year I would breakout with something new and have a Women's Conference called "Am I My

Sister's Keeper?" "Yes, I Am". That is what He gave me to move forward in hosting my first women's conference in 2018. If that wasn't enough of the new things to come, I had this vision to start my own YouTube TV Show. I tried putting something out there on my own, but that didn't work out so well. Then I connected with a friend named Tom who is a retired TV producer. He agreed to volunteer his time giving back and helping young students learn video and production skills. Tom and I connected where we will be running a program with students to help produce my new TV show called "Here To Connect School and Community", and it will be featured on the Phoenixville local community channel.

Chapter 7
I'm Sixty, Sassy and.....Single

Life is exciting and painful, and I'm embracing it all!

I am Sixty, Sassy and Single and in my third quarter of life. GOD has blessed my journey through lots of SHIPS and being able to reflect on all the relationships in life has been amazing. I am very grateful and thankful for the support and time I have had. We should not take the family, friends and community we have in our lives for granted. I said it before and I'll say it again, I realize the choice I made not to get married was for a reason. I am the Bride of Christ, and He said to "Be Satisfied with Me". I would not have been able to bless so many people and accomplish so many things, and I do believe that with my whole heart. I have been satisfied with living in my purpose and passion helping and serving

254

others. So many people live wishing they would have done this or that, but there are no regrets for me. I never allowed my heart to be given to anyone without truly committing my total self to them, and I have always been faithful in my relationships. Turning 60 this year is huge for me. Being sixty is something to be proud of. Football is my favorite sport, and I'm in the third quarter of my life. I'm very excited about my future and where GOD is taking me. I'm "Sixty, Sassy, Single and waiting to be Found". I continue to be Healthy, Happy and Hopeful in pursing my dreams, and in my pursuit, I am satisfied with HIM!

BE SATISFIED WITH ME
By St. Anthony of Padua

Everyone longs to give themselves
completely to someone,
To have a deep soul relationship with another,
to be loved thoroughly and exclusively.
But to a Christian, God says,
"No, not until you are satisfied,
fulfilled and content with being loved by Me alone,
with giving yourself totally & unreservedly to Me,
with having an intensely personal and unique
relationship with Me alone.
Discovering that only in Me
is your satisfaction to be found,
will you be capable of the perfect human
relationship that I have planned for you.
You will never be united to another
until you are united with Me.
Exclusive of anyone or anything else.
Exclusive of any other desires or longings.
I want you to stop planning, stop wishing,
and allow Me to give you the most thrilling plan
existing . . . one you cannot imagine.
I want you to have the best.
Please allow Me to bring it to you.
You just keep watching Me,
expecting the greatest things.
Keep experiencing the satisfaction that I AM.
Keep listening & learning the things that I tell you.
Just wait, that's all. Don't be anxious, Don't worry
Don't look around at things others have gotten
Or that I have given them.

Don't look around at the things
you think you want,
Just keep looking off and away up to Me,
or you'll miss what I want to show you.
And then, when you're ready,
I'll surprise you with a love
far more wonderful than you could dream of.

You see, until you are ready, and until the one
I have for you is ready,
I am working even at this moment
to have both of you ready at the same time.
Until you are both satisfied exclusively with Me
and the life I prepared for you,
You won't be able to experience the love that
exemplified your relationship with Me.
And this is perfect love.
And dear one, I want you to have this
most wonderful love,
I want you to see in the flesh a picture
of your relationship with Me.
And to enjoy materially and concretely
the everlasting union of beauty, perfection & love
that I offer you with Myself.
Know that I love you utterly. I AM God.
Believe it and be satisfied.

When I read this poem for the first time,
It encouraged me and gave me new
perspective.
I made a resolution to keep looking to God
and finding happiness in Him.

CHAPTER 8
Here To Connect

I want to leave you with Here To Connect. I hope that I was able to connect to you. The most important thing that you will treasure in life is the relationships you have had. When you attend someone's home going services, it is never how many material things you have possessed, but how many lives have you touched. I say that I want flowers while I am living. At my home going service only candles lit to symbolize the light I have shown. Let my life be that light that can live on through the relationships and people who I have helped along my life's journey. That is what truly living life is all about. You choose your path and the people you allow to be a part of your ship. Who will you let aboard your ship to sail and ride the waves that life will send your way? Make sure you surround yourself with people who bring out the best in who you are and are

moving in a positive way. Living is giving –
Giving comes before living. You get to know
that as you travel life's journey.

Know Thyself

I have to live with myself,
and so I want to be fit for myself.
To know I want to be able as years go by
always to look at myself in the eye.
I don't want to stand with the setting sun,
and hate myself for the things I've done.
I don't want to keep on the closet shelf
a lot of secrets about myself,
and fool myself as I come and go
thinking nobody else will know
the kind of person I really am.
I don't want to dress up in shame,
I can never hide myself from me.
I see what others may never know.
I can never fool myself and, so,
through the struggle for fame and wealth,
I want to be able to like myself.
I don't want to look at myself and know
that I'm a blustery and blunt
and empty show.
I want to go out with my head erect.
I want to endure all people's respect.
And whatever happens, I want to be
self-respected and conscience free.

Behavior is a choice. Who do you spend the most time with and who is talking into your life, meaning the influences who surround you. If they have thoughts, feelings or actions, they know they have power to shape your life. People are either raising you up or pulling you down. Hang around people who have what you want. Creating a winning mindset and watching what you are listening to has the power to control what direction you will be taking in life. Four words I work on not using are try, when, worry, and can't. I call it no sinking thinking. The number one thing that will help change your life is to change your thinking. What you have to speak into existence is "Believing It Can Happen!" Words are so important. What we have learned from that is once you say the words, you can't take them back. If they are hurtful, it is like cutting someone. The bleeding stops and the scars heal but you still have the scar. It will take forgiving yourself to move forward and have peace in your life. What you speak will show up in life. Getting your heart and mind aligned is the key. Your feelings drive your thoughts. What you put out is what you get back. Try to stay focused, look for opportunities in all situations, and wake to see the reason for the blessings that will come your way. Everything happens for a reason. You just have to push through to the finish line. "May the words of my mouth and the meditation of my heart be acceptable in Your sight, O Lord." Psalm 19:14

Suggested scriptures to help you control our tongue: Matthew 5:33-37, 12:34-37, and Ephesians 4:29

Making different choices... Are you ready???

Let's get started with some new goals for improvement in your life. Using the words listed below, write something next to them about an area of your life that you are willing to change.

Business

Family

Fitness

Finances

Health

Money

Relationships

Spirituality

If you are able to believe in your goals, you will be able to achieve them. Remember it is in the mindset.

Awareness..... What are you doing? What are you not doing? Do Something?

Who gives energy and who takes it away?

Spouse/Significant Other

Children

Friends

Family

Colleagues

Manager/Supervisor

Staff

Teacher/Advisor

Other

A lot depends on you. Stop the hating and start participating!

What would you do if you were not afraid of failing? Get out of the way and let the miracles begin in your life.

Ask yourself this question, Am I Happy? If not, what would I need to make me happy? The answers to these questions will pull out of your heart and mind where you are in life. Assessing our lives will give us the opportunity to improve the quality of our lives while still living.

I agree with Dale Carneige, Author and Writer about happiness and the meaning of a smile. Happiness to me is waking each morning in fellowship with GOD, having a smile on my face and realizing how blessed I am to be safe and secure, have my health, and having my family supporting me in my dreams and goals in life. When I get up, I start my day with excitement and expectation of what GOD is going to do. I ask GOD to use me as a vessel to bless someone today. Sometimes it only takes a smile to bless someone. I want to share his message about the meaning of a smile. It cost nothing. It creates much. It enriches those who receive without impoverishing those who give. It happens in a flash, and the memory of it sometimes lasts forever. There are none so rich that they can get along without it, and none so poor but are richer for its benefits. It creates happiness in the home, fosters good will in business, and is the countersign of friends. It is rest to the weary, daylight to the discouraged, sunshine to the sad and nature's best antidote for the trouble. And, yet, it cannot be begged, borrowed or stolen. For it is something that is no earthly good to anyone until it is given away. So in the course of the day, your friends may be too tried to give a smile. Then why don't you give them one of yours because nobody needs a smile more than those who have none left to give. SMILE! Bless someone today with your smile! That is one of my favorite thing to do each day. You have no idea what someone is facing. If the world would allow this to become contagious, lots of people would feel just a little bit better to get through the day.

These are the tools that helped me to assess my life and make changes in it. I developed a 90 Day Plan to make change for who and what I would have in my life. I picked 4 Key areas and started the process. I developed an action plan that included the support I needed and the help of a mentor.

I am a part of the "Me Too" Movement. It happened to me too! I am choosing to focus on the "We Movement" with "Here To Connect Movement for Women & Girls". My mission of creating a system that connects women and girls in an accountable partnership, friendship and relationship through fellowship and being supportive helps each of them accomplish their dreams and goals while bonding with each other. This movement provides an atmosphere of inclusion and inspiration for every women and girl. Women will have the opportunity to create connections and leave with a stronger sense of how to connect, who to connect to, and why connecting with other women and girls is important to our sense of self at home and throughout our communities. They will also have access to a wealth of tangible information that will enhance their personal and professional growth.

To be successful and happy in life, you must have wishbone, backbone and a funny bone.

I learned to be patient because GOD's delays are not always denials. HE knows what's best for us and, in His time, HE will supply all your needs. I believe that with ALL MY HEART! The Secret of True Love is learning "We love because He first loved us." (1 John 4:19); Obedience - "For this is love for GOD, to obey His commands." (1 John 5:3a); Victory - "...everyone born of GOD overcomes the world. And this is the victory that has overcome the world: our faith..." (1 John 5:3b-4); Empowerment - "And we know that in all things GOD works for the good for those who love Him, who have been called according to

267

His purpose. For I am convinced that neither the present, nor the future, nor any powers, nor height, nor depth, nor anything else in all creation will be able to separate us from the love of GOD that is in Christ Jesus our Lord." (Romans 8:28-29)

LOVE IS VERY SPECIAL – Shining Star 1991

Anytime is such a nice time
To think of those we know;
Friends and neighbors whom we meet
Seem to have an extra glow.
Love is very special
But it never becomes love
Until it's given freely
With God's blessings from above.
When we clothe our thoughts in love
And send them forth to bless,
We find each little thought or word
Comes back to our address.
When we imbue our hours with love
At home, at work, at school
We find we have more pleasant days
Because we're following God's rule.
So let's just each affirm this day
And pray to God above
That in all we do, we'll do our best
To bless people with our love.

Being less than the Best
If you don't distance yourself from the wrong
people,
you will never meet the right people.
Keeping your thoughts in the right direction,
now is the time to step into your destiny.
You are on the run way to taking off.
God will connect the dots.
Anything that you are going through
will be useful in life.
God will use all of your disappointments in
your life to help you become strong.
We were made to give.
I am grateful to know You.
You are my heart beat.

Is There Any Hope?
The future is uncertain.
Families are falling apart.
Drugs are ruining cities and schools.
Disease is killing our people.
Is There any Hope?
Can we have peace and joy in our hearts?
Can we have fulfillment in life?
Can we have power and strength
to live meaningful lives?
Does anyone really care?
YES! Here's Hope: JESUS Cares for YOU

The Bible says:
"Now may the God of hope fill you with all joy and peace in believing; that you may abound in hope, by the power of the Holy Spirit" (Romans 15:13).

The Bible is our guide for living comfort when you are in trouble. Strength for your faith. Rest when you are weary. How to cope with worry. How to forgive and be forgiven. How to pray The Beatitudes. The meaning of love. The Christmas Story. The Story of Easter. The return of Christ. The description of Heaven. Read 2 Timothy 3:14-17, John 14:1-18, Hebrews 11:1-40, Matthew 11:25-30, Matthew 6:24-34, Matthew 18:21-35, Matthew 6:5-13, Matthew 5:3-12, 1 Corinthians 13:1-13, Luke 2:1-20, Luke 24:1-10, 1 Thessalonians 4:13-18, and Revelation 21:1-17.

You Are Assured of Eternal Life & Hope Because:

You can trust God's promise: "Whoever will call upon the name of the Lord will be saved" (Romans 10:13). Did you sincerely ask Jesus into your heart as Lord and Savior? Where is He right now? What does God's Word promise? • You are a member of God's family. The Spirit Himself bears witness with our spirit, that we are children of God" (Romans 8:16). • Your life is eternally secure in God. "For I am convinced that neither death, nor life, nor angels, nor principalities, nor things present, nor things to come, nor powers, nor height, nor depth, nor any other created thing, shall be able to separate us from the love of God, which is in Christ Jesus our Lord." (Romans 8:38-39).

What Happens After You Receive Hope from God? • You will begin to live for God (Romans 12:1-2, 9-18. • You will publicly profess your faith by being baptized (Matthew 18:19-20; Luke 3:21, Romans 6:4). • You will share with others what Jesus has done for you (Romans 10:14). • You will get to know God better through prayer, Bible study, and fellowship with other Christians as a member of a local church (Romans 15:4-6).

Women are Lost Treasures
By Paul Jenkins

Women have strengths that should amaze men.
They bear hardships and they carry burdens.
They hold happiness, love and joy.
They smile when they want to scream.
They sing when they want to cry.
They cry when they are happy and laugh when
they are nervous.
They fight for what they believe in.

They stand up to injustice.
They don't take "No" for an answer
when they believe there is a better solution.
They go without so their family can have.
They go to the doctor with a frightened friend.
They love unconditionally.
They cry when their children excel and cheer
when their friends get awards.
They are happy when they hear about a birth
or a wedding.
Their heart breaks when a friend dies.
They grieve at the loss of a family member,
yet they are strong when they think there is
no strength left.
They know that a hug and a kiss
can heal a broken heart.
Women come in all shapes, sizes and colors.
They'll drive, fly, walk or run to show how much
they care about you.
The heart of a woman is what makes the world
keep turning.
They bring joy, hope and love.
They have compassion and ideals.
They give moral support to their family
and friends.
Women have vital things to say
and everything to give.

HOWEVER, WOMEN HAVE ONE FLAW, THEY FORGET THEIR WORTH!

Why would you want to write a book, people ask me? I say it's because I want to share all the blessings I had and have in my life to help others learn what I learned, that if you dream big, stay on the positive path, and allow the right people in your life, you too could have a journey that you want to share with others. We do not know the day, time or hour GOD will take us home, so I live life like it is my last day. I'm enjoying the journey (ETJ) as my ship keeps sailing along, and I am building my life while believing in my CAPTAIN to steer me in the right direction. I have so many great projects that I am working on, and I am praying that my life's journey will have touched someone's life and they'll realize that GOD is the source that will help your dreams come true. HE will put people in your life to help you. Your fellowship with Him creates the spiritual energy that will draw others to you, and that will help you develop relationships you'll need along the way. That is the key to success. You cannot do it alone. I hope that my book has shed some light on the importance of relationships, friendships, mentorships, partnerships, championships, leadership and fellowship. Without fellowship, none of these ships will sail smoothly. Surround yourself with people who will help you fulfill your dreams. My future holds greater things to come. The next series from Dolly Dishes It Out will be "Chosen Sister, Ask Me Why". I hope you have enjoyed each slice of my life. Get ready while I am cooking up my next dish.

Reference Books

Walk Tall - Affirmations for People of Color by Carleen Brice. RPI Publishing Co, San Diego, California

Think And Grow Rich, A Black Choice - Dennis Kimbro and Napoleon Hill - Fawcett. Columbine Balantine Books, New York, NY

It's About Time- *Getting Control of Life* - Ken Smith, Foreword by Larry Burkett. Living Books, Tyndale House Publishing, Inc., Wheaton Illinois

How to Succeed in Business Without Being White, Foreword by Robert C. Crandall. Earl Graves Publisher & CEO of Black Enterprise Magazine

40 Days with Jesus, Celebrating His Presence, Sarah Young. Copyright by Sarah Young

Don't Sweat the Small Stuff....and it's all small stuff - Richard Carlson P.H. D. Coauthor of Handbook for The Soul

Season of Life, Jeffrey Marx - Copyright by Jeffrey Marx

Are You Listening? Hearing His Word, Doing His Will? Gloria Copeland. Published by Harrison House, Inc, Tulsa Oklahoma

The Dream Manager, Matthew Kelly, with a Foreword by Patrick Lencioni. Beacon Publishing

Sweet Expectations Michele Hoskins Recipe for Success, Adams Media F&W Publishing Co., Avon, MA

How to Connect

Here is my contact information:

Phone: 484-378-6116

Email: heretoapparel.com

LinkedIn: Dolores Winston

Facebook: My Personal Page

Facebook: Dolores Winston, Author
@DollyDishesItOut

Facebook: My Here to Connect Page

Websites: www.heretoapparel.com
www.heretowinapparel.com

Looking forward to connecting with YOU!

Dolores Winston has been a beacon of light for this community. Her warmth, her creativity and especially her enthusiasm, inspires those around her, propelling them to take the risks necessary to become all they can be. Were it not for Dolores, this community would be greatly diminished.

All the best,
Greg Porter
The Daniel Foundation

Dolly has had a varied and interesting life, full of highs and lows. Regardless of what happens to her, she is always a paragon of prayer and grace. Her life is worth reading about, pondering over and emulating.

Dorene Pasekof
Hill Creek Farm

Over the last decade, I have had the privilege to develop a bond with Dolores that started out as a community service networking opportunity, and it has turned into a life-long friendship. We had a mutual passion for helping children in our community overcome some very adverse circumstances and keep them connected to daily activities. Her passion for helping others has birthed several businesses within her community. She is always thinking of others and is now focusing on herself. I am so happy that she finally gets to share her vision and voice with so many more than just those in her community because her message has something for everyone.

Monique Henderson, M.S., Ed. S., CSP
The Zoeza Afya Group, P.C.

I met Dolores Winston (affectionately known as Dolly) when we were teenagers. We are the same age. Dolly and I worked at a factory in Oaks, PA. I was calm and quiet, and Dolly was very talkative and outgoing. That being said, we were a perfect match and became fast friends. Dolly and I have been good friends ever since. Even though we would go months at a time without communicating, we always picked right back up where we were as if it were yesterday.

I have watched Dolly grow into a mature woman. If asked, "What are the qualities you see in Dolly?" I would reply that Dolly loves God, she loves her family and she loves life. Dolly remains very enthusiastic to this day. What I mean by that is, Dolly allows the Holy Spirit to be evident in her life. She gives testimony to God's goodness and favor. She pursues her goals and aspirations. Not only does she pursue her goals, Dolly achieves them. Throughout her life, she has won many awards and she is very deserving of these honors. She does not boast about her achievements but gives all of the glory to God. She knows that God has a plan for her life, and she is obedient in following his plan.

Dolly is dedicated to her family and friends. She is proud when she speaks of them and is always there when she is needed. Dolly is a mentor to many in the community and helps young men and women aspire to be better people. Dolly sees the good in each person and helps them to see the good in themselves and realize their full potential.

In her business, "Here to Apparel", the theme is "Here to _____". It is inspiring in that we all have a purpose. Living a purposeful life means that we could be *Here to Win, Here to Love, Here to Give, Here to Receive, Here to Honor* and so forth. Dolly's theme tells us that we must be purposeful in our actions because we are all here to do something. Dolly knows and demonstrates that it is better to give then to receive. She is always ready and present which exemplifies the "Here to" theme.

In closing, I would like to say that Dolly Winston has many big goals and aspirations, and I have no doubt that all of her goals will be achieved. I will not tell you what her aspirations and goals are, just keep watching and see what God will do with her life. Stay tuned. The best is yet to come!!

Doreen Bearden

When I was asked by Dolores "Dolly" Winston to write a few words for her book, I was deeply honored. I thought this would certainly be easy because there are so many wonderful things that I can say about her. However, this was not as easy a task as I thought. It is not that Dolly is complicated. Actually, she is a simple, humble, loving person who, at the very core of her being, sees the good in everyone. But I wanted to tell you how I came to know and see these things in her.

I first met Dolly when I was principal at one of the elementary schools and was asked by the Superintendent of the school district to serve as his district representative on the Social Concerns Committee. Dolly had just been welcomed as a new member of the organization.

It was a friendship that began immediately based on a mutual love for the school district, community, and our God. Together we planned prayer breakfasts, inclusivity meetings, and opportunities for community dialog. And we sang together whenever we had the chance!

Through the years, I watched Dolly grow and flourish as she searched to add more meaning to her life, both spiritually and intellectually. I am so very proud of this amazing mother, grandmother, community leader, and now, author, for all that she has accomplished. My love and friendship go with you always, Dolly, wherever your journey takes you.

Karen W. Coldwell, Ed. D.

Dolly Winston lights up a room. There isn't a more enthusiastic or passionate person around! Her energy is electric and contagious, and her will is strong and righteous. She uses both to get done the things that she believes in. And she chooses to believe in things that work to make our world a better, more just, more unified and more loving place.

Dolly bravely ventures forward in places where she could resist and play it safe – and with each new venture she expands not just herself but the people around her that go on the ride with her. I have been privileged to watch her apply herself to a number of things. I was most closely involved in watching her take a hurting non-profit organization and turn it around and not just by sheer force of will, but through intelligence, skill and wisdom too. I feel very lucky that my path crossed with Dolly's decades ago, and I continue to watch her as every day she relentlessly and creatively works to bring people together across racial, financial, political and other divides for the betterment of us all. Thank you, Dolly.

Moira Mumma
Citizen Advocacy

Dolly gives it to us real! Treat yourself today to a fresh, surprising and delicious book about success and how *the rest of us* can obtain it! Hint: it's not in the getting, it's in the giving!"

Nina M. Guzman

FRIENDSHIP
I first met Dolores Winston in the Fall of 2001. As a community health nurse, I was to be the outreach nurse for a weekly program beginning at Bethel Baptist Church, "Aim for Healthy Ways" (AHW). The goal of the program was to educate and promote healthy living for the members of the church and

283

surrounding community. During my first AHW patient session, I was introduced to Dolores, better known as Dolly, the church member and community leader who had partnered with our community hospital to make AHW a reality.

From the start, Dolly was friendly, supportive and anxious to do whatever would make AHW work. From that moment on, we developed a friendship thru caring—caring about our community. Along the way, we took time to enjoy the rides.

Since 2001, I have watched my friend continue to develop community programming that made positive changes. Her energies are enormous and her ideas never cease. At times, I stand by the wayside and marvel. If I had one wish for Dolly, I would ask that she continues to be well and motivated in making her dreams come true for the community she loves.

Billie Goldstein

Dolly, your story reflects the successes and challenges that we all encounter in our lives. We celebrate your entrepreneurial spirit, service to the community, and religious faith knowing that these things have been a source of encouragement for and an example to others.

Shaped by a narrative that emerges out of family, community and faith, and your own life experiences so that others from your story can find their own way to a meaningful life of action and service on behalf of others. You have proven yourself to be a friend, mentor, sponsor, and woman of GOD to many people.

We sit at Dolly's table to feast as she "dishes out" inspiring stories and food for thought.

God's blessings to you and the success of your book!

Reverend Nathan Coleman, Pastor
Bethel Baptist Church, Phoenixville PA

To a woman who has refused to let her past dictate her future. A woman who has been there for many with inspiration and deeds. Much Love Cuz.

DeNeal Saunders

Behind every growing and thriving community are leaders who have the unwavering, dependable and thoughtful fortitude to make sure all are served and all benefit from the evolution of the community. Dolores "Dolly" Winston is one of these leaders. Her care, understanding, commitment, desire and dedication to the Phoenixville community and her church have made many noteworthy differences in the lives of so many in the community. She embodies and pushes us all. Her life and theme is *Together We Can*. As the Superintendent of Schools for the Phoenixville Area School District, I applaud and thank her for her courage, care and commitment to the Phoenixville community. While takes a village to raise a child, it takes leadership to lead a community. Dolly is a leader.

Alan D. Fegley, Ed.D.
Superintendent of Schools
Phoenixville Area School District

In 2015 I met a warm, generous woman of faith with an electrifying, infectious personality by the name of Dolores Winston. Affectionately known by friends and family as Dolly. We shared a breakfast table while attending Black Enterprise Entrepreneurs Conference in Atlanta, GA. Our conversation was easy and genuine. Immediately I knew she and I would become lifelong friends. Last October I attended an Expo Event she hosted to honor Women Veterans, and Female Entrepreneurs in her hometown of Phoenixville, PA. The event was a success and so is Dolly! Don't be fooled by her Southern charm because she is not a newbie to the entrepreneurial world. She wears many, many hats; former owner of Dolly's Dish Restaurant. She still caters her downhome cooking and mouthwatering Sweet Potato Pies for numerous area events. Her Sweet Potato Pies leave you begging for more... She is the C.E.O. of Here to Apparel, LLC, Vice President of Phoenixville Area Positive Alternatives (PAPA) a non-profit community-based organization that offers year-round academic, athletic, and personal enrichment programs for students in the Phoenixville Area School District. Dolly pretty much does it all! New challenges fuel her ambitions. Her ever growing portfolio now includes author. She has written a Memoir *entitled Dolly*

Dishes It Out She's Sixty, Sassy, Single and Waiting to Be Found. I was privileged to have a sneak preview and already made a prediction that it will be a #1 Bestseller. When you begin reading Dolly Dishes It Out... this heartwarming page turner will real you in and you won't be able to put it down. Dolly opens up her heart and bares her soul as she invites us into intimate, corners of her life. *Dolly Dishes It Out...* has a surprise twist you won't see coming. Dolly is already setting big goals for this project. She has her sights set on an interview with her favorite celebrity Entrepreneur, Talk Show, Radio and Family Feud Game Show Host Steve Harvey, a Super Soul Sunday book interview with Mega Celebrity, Entrepreneur, Media Mogul, Philanthropist, Oprah Winfrey and a collaborative movie project with Entrepreneur, Actor, Movie, and T.V. Writer, Director, Producer Mogul Tyler Perry. Wow! Sounds ambitious, right? Not for the little can-do dynamo I've come to know and love. Not only does Dolly talk about what she wants to do, she makes them happen! All I can say is stay tuned to see what she will be dishing up next. No matter what it is you can count on it being a winner!

Cheryl Ketchens, Best-selling Author
C.E.O. of Wellness Is Power, LLC